Civil Liberties

Other Books of Related Interest

Opposing Viewpoints Series

Church and State
Democracy
Judicial Activism

At Issue Series

Alternatives to Prisons
Do Children Have Rights?
Guns and Crime
Should Religious Symbols Be Allowed on Public Land?

Current Controversies Series

Teens and Privacy

"Congress shall make no law … abridging the freedom of speech, or of the press."

First Amendment to the US Constitution

The basic foundation of our democracy is the First Amendment guarantee of freedom of expression. The Opposing Viewpoints Series is dedicated to the concept of this basic freedom and the idea that it is more important to practice it than to enshrine it.

OPPOSING
VIEWPOINTS®
SERIES

| Civil Liberties

Noël Merino, Book Editor

GREENHAVEN PRESS
A part of Gale, Cengage Learning

GALE
CENGAGE Learning·

Detroit • New York • San Francisco • New Haven, Conn • Waterville, Maine • London

GALE
CENGAGE Learning

Elizabeth Des Chenes, *Director, Publishing Solutions*

© 2013 Greenhaven Press, a part of Gale, Cengage Learning

Gale and Greenhaven Press are registered trademarks used herein under license.

For more information, contact:
Greenhaven Press
27500 Drake Rd.
Farmington Hills, MI 48331-3535
Or you can visit our Internet site at gale.cengage.com.

For product information and technology assistance, contact us at:

Gale Customer Support, 1-800-877-4253.
For permission to use material from this text or product, submit all requests online at www.cengage.com/permissions.

Further permissions questions can be emailed to permissionrequest@cengage.com.

Articles in Greenhaven Press anthologies are often edited for length to meet page requirements. In addition, original titles of these works are changed to clearly present the main thesis and to explicitly indicate the author's opinion. Every effort is made to ensure that Greenhaven Press accurately reflects the original intent of the authors. Every effort has been made to trace the owners of copyrighted material.

Cover Image © justasc/Shutterstock.com.

LIBRARY OF CONGRESS CATALOGING-IN-PUBLICATION DATA

Civil liberties / Noël Merino, book editor.
    pages cm. -- (Opposing viewpoints)
    Includes bibliographical references and index.
    ISBN 978-0-7377-6304-1 (hardcover) -- ISBN 978-0-7377-6305-8 (softcover)
 1. Civil rights--United States--Juvenile literature. I. Merino, Noël. editor of compilation.
    KF4750.C491 2013
    342.7308'5--dc23

                                                                    2013001147

Printed in the United States of America
1 2 3 4 5 6 7 17 16 15 14 13

Contents

Chapter 3: Is the Right to Due Process in Danger?

Chapter 4: Is the Right to Privacy in Jeopardy?

Why Consider Opposing Viewpoints?

> *"The only way in which a human being can make some approach to knowing the whole of a subject is by hearing what can be said about it by persons of every variety of opinion and studying all modes in which it can be looked at by every character of mind. No wise man ever acquired his wisdom in any mode but this."*
>
> John Stuart Mill

In our media-intensive culture it is not difficult to find differing opinions. Thousands of newspapers and magazines and dozens of radio and television talk shows resound with differing points of view. The difficulty lies in deciding which opinion to agree with and which "experts" seem the most credible. The more inundated we become with differing opinions and claims, the more essential it is to hone critical reading and thinking skills to evaluate these ideas. Opposing Viewpoints books address this problem directly by presenting stimulating debates that can be used to enhance and teach these skills. The varied opinions contained in each book examine many different aspects of a single issue. While examining these conveniently edited opposing views, readers can develop critical thinking skills such as the ability to compare and contrast authors' credibility, facts, argumentation styles, use of persuasive techniques, and other stylistic tools. In short, the Opposing Viewpoints Series is an ideal way to attain the higher-level thinking and reading skills so essential in a culture of diverse and contradictory opinions.

In addition to providing a tool for critical thinking, Opposing Viewpoints books challenge readers to question their own strongly held opinions and assumptions. Most people form their opinions on the basis of upbringing, peer pressure, and personal, cultural, or professional bias. By reading carefully balanced opposing views, readers must directly confront new ideas as well as the opinions of those with whom they disagree. This is not to argue simplistically that everyone who reads opposing views will—or should—change his or her opinion. Instead, the series enhances readers' understanding of their own views by encouraging confrontation with opposing ideas. Careful examination of others' views can lead to the readers' understanding of the logical inconsistencies in their own opinions, perspective on why they hold an opinion, and the consideration of the possibility that their opinion requires further evaluation.

Evaluating Other Opinions

To ensure that this type of examination occurs, Opposing Viewpoints books present all types of opinions. Prominent spokespeople on different sides of each issue as well as well-known professionals from many disciplines challenge the reader. An additional goal of the series is to provide a forum for other, less known, or even unpopular viewpoints. The opinion of an ordinary person who has had to make the decision to cut off life support from a terminally ill relative, for example, may be just as valuable and provide just as much insight as a medical ethicist's professional opinion. The editors have two additional purposes in including these less known views. One, the editors encourage readers to respect others' opinions—even when not enhanced by professional credibility. It is only by reading or listening to and objectively evaluating others' ideas that one can determine whether they are worthy of consideration. Two, the inclusion of such viewpoints encourages the important critical thinking skill of objectively evaluating an author's credentials and bias. This evaluation will illuminate an author's reasons for taking a particular stance on an issue and will aid in readers' evaluation of the author's ideas.

It is our hope that these books will give readers a deeper understanding of the issues debated and an appreciation of the complexity of even seemingly simple issues when good and honest people disagree. This awareness is particularly important in a democratic society such as ours in which people enter into public debate to determine the common good. Those with whom one disagrees should not be regarded as enemies but rather as people whose views deserve careful examination and may shed light on one's own.

Thomas Jefferson once said that "difference of opinion leads to inquiry, and inquiry to truth." Jefferson, a broadly educated man, argued that "if a nation expects to be ignorant and free . . . it expects what never was and never will be." As individuals and as a nation, it is imperative that we consider the opinions of others and examine them with skill and discernment. The Opposing Viewpoints Series is intended to help readers achieve this goal.

David L. Bender and Bruno Leone,
Founders

Introduction

"A bill of rights is what the people are
entitled to against every government on
earth, general or particular, and what
no just government should refuse."
Thomas Jefferson, Letter to James
Madison, December 20, 1787

Civil liberties are rights and freedoms held by individuals and protected by government. The civil liberties of Americans are primarily found in the Bill of Rights. The Bill of Rights was adopted in 1791 in response to demand for greater explicit protection of individual rights. At the United States Constitutional Convention in 1787, several delegates refused to sign the Constitution without such explicit protection. In 1789 Congress passed the Bill of Rights, which comprises the first ten amendments to the Constitution and which went into effect in 1791 after ratification by three-fourths of the states, according to law.

The philosophical underpinning for civil liberties in the United States can be traced to respect for the natural rights of humans. Several Enlightenment thinkers helped these ideas to flourish. The thinking of seventeenth-century English philosopher John Locke, often considered the founder of classic liberal philosophy, is often credited as influencing the Founding Fathers of the United States. A proponent of natural rights, in his *Second Treatise of Government* he writes:

The state of nature has a law of nature to govern it, which obliges every one: and reason, which is that law, teaches all mankind, who will but consult it, that being all equal and independent, no one ought to harm another in his life, health, liberty, or possessions.[1]

His reasoning here is often thought to have influenced the Declaration of Independence, which states:

> We hold these truths to be self-evident, that all men are created equal, that they are endowed by their creator with certain unalienable Rights, that among these are Life, Liberty and the pursuit of Happiness.

Locke proposed that the function of a legitimate government is to defend the natural rights to life, health, liberty, and property of its citizens. The demand for the Bill of Rights was a demand to specifically declare in the Constitution the foundational liberties accorded to citizens.

Within the Bill of Rights are protections for several civil liberties. The First Amendment guarantees freedom of expression and religious freedom. The Fourth Amendment protects persons, including their homes and possessions, from unreasonable searches and seizures, providing a strong basis for a right to privacy. The Fifth, Sixth, and Eighth Amendments provide protections for due process during criminal procedures. Subsequent amendments explicitate these rights; for example, the Fourteenth Amendment, adopted in 1868, extends the protection of civil liberties from federal government restriction to protection from state government infringement as well.

While there is not widespread controversy over the content of the Bill of Rights, there is plenty of debate concerning how it ought to be interpreted. The liberties identified in the Bill of Rights are by no means absolute and in some cases the limit of certain liberties is clear. For example, individuals are free to express criticism of government, but issuing a death threat to a government official is a type of expression that could be seen as a criminal offense. Individuals are free to attend a church of their choosing, but freedom of religion does not protect the right to practice human sacrifice, even for religious reasons. Law enforcement officers may search an individual without an official warrant if they have a strong justification for believing that individual may have committed an act of terrorism, but police may not create a roadblock to search everyone in town in order to find their suspect. One has the expectation in the privacy of one's home to not have one's picture taken, but at a ballgame no such guarantee exists.

In other situations, however, drawing the line where a liberty ends is not nearly as clear. Scholars and commentators have addressed issues such as whether the expression of racial hatred should be criminalized; whether religious freedom allows public-school teachers to talk about God; whether law enforcement may assassinate terrorist suspects on foreign soil; and when concerns about security trump the right to privacy. Topics such as these illustrate that it is not always clear when it is justified to restrain civil liberties; concerns about harm to others and national security need to be balanced with concerns about individual rights. Numerous debates and perspectives are explored in *Opposing Viewpoints: Civil Liberties,* in chapters titled: Should Limits Be Placed on Freedom of Expression?, Does the First Amendment Require Separation of Church and State?, Is the Right to Due Process in Danger?, and Is the Right to Privacy in Jeopardy?

Note

1. John Locke, *Second Treatise of Government,* 1690.

CHAPTER 1

Should Limits Be Placed on Freedom of Expression?

Chapter Preface

Freedom of expression is one of the most valued civil liberties in the United States. Protected by the US Constitution, the First Amendment guarantees that "Congress shall make no law . . . abridging the freedom of speech, or of the press; or the right of the people peaceably to assemble, and to petition the Government for a redress of grievances." The freedoms of speech, press, assembly, and petition collectively constitute freedom of expression in the United States, with the understanding that freedom of expression is not limited to speech and can include symbolic expression. However, this freedom has never been interpreted to be absolute, and not all forms of expression are constitutionally protected. Exactly what kinds of expression the First Amendment protects is an issue that has frequently made its way to court, and the US Supreme Court has made several key decisions over the years that have determined how the First Amendment is to be interpreted.

In 1942, a unanimous Supreme Court defined several categories of speech that are not protected by the First Amendment:

> There are certain well defined and narrowly limited classes of speech, the prevention and punishment of which have never been thought to raise any Constitutional problem. These include the lewd and obscene, the profane, the libelous, and the insulting or "fighting" words—those which, by their very utterance, inflict injury or tend to incite an immediate breach of the peace. It has been well observed that such utterances are no essential part of any exposition of ideas, and are of such slight social value as a step to truth that any benefit that may be derived from them is clearly outweighed by the social interest in order and morality.[1]

Three broad categories of unprotected speech stand out: speech that is obscene, speech that publicly defames another person, and speech that tends to incite lawlessness. These restrictions have been progressively loosened over the last few decades.

In 1964, the Supreme Court weakened restrictions on libel for public officials, requiring that limits on defamation only apply when there is "reckless disregard of whether it was false or not."[2] In 1969, the Court tightened the definition of speech that incites lawlessness to that which is intended to produce "imminent lawless action."[3] Thus, expression advocating lawlessness is not itself prohibited unless the speaker intends to incite lawlessness when it is both about to occur and likely to do so. And in 1973, the Court established a test for whether expression is deemed obscene and thus not protected by the First Amendment: The basic guidelines for the trier of fact must be: (a) whether "the average person, applying contemporary community standards" would find that the work, taken as a whole, appeals to the prurient interest; (b) whether the work depicts or describes, in a patently offensive way, sexual conduct specifically defined by the applicable state law; and (c) whether the work, taken as a whole, lacks serious literary, artistic, political, or scientific value.[4] Although material that is deemed obscene can be subject to limits on distribution and sale, personal use and possession has not been ruled to be unconstitutional. The standard of the so-called *Miller* test has been criticized for being overly vague and too dependent on local norms.

The constitutional protection of freedom of expression in the United States is strong, but it is not absolute. When the value of allowing expression is outweighed by the harm it causes, there may be grounds to restrict such expression. Arguments on both sides of the issue, however, can be fierce, and a resolution for or against the protection of expression is not always clear. A sampling of some of the most controversial issues—hate speech, corporate political expression, and expression on the Internet—are considered in this chapter.

Notes

1. *Chaplinsky v. Stage of New Hampshire*, 1942.
2. *New York Times Co. v. Sulllivan*, 1964.
3. *Brandenberg v. Ohio*, 1969.
4. *Miller v. California*, 1973.

"Proscribing hate speech more broadly would, I believe, foster a more inclusive, tolerant, and safer society."

Hate Speech Should Be Criminalized

Joyce Arthur

In the following viewpoint, Joyce Arthur argues that hate speech should not be protected by the right to freedom of expression. Arthur claims that speech used to disparage a person or group of persons has no social benefit and can cause harm. She contends that hate speech can play a role in inspiring individuals to violence, and she believes that not only should perpetrators of violence be prosecuted but also those who influence the perpetrators by expressing hate. Arthur is the founder and executive director of the Abortion Rights Coalition of Canada, a national political pro-choice group.

As you read, consider the following questions:

1. According to Arthur, in the United States hate speech is protected under the First Amendment unless it constitutes what?

2. According to the author, what is the most popular solution to the problem of free speech, with which she disagrees?
3. What right does Arthur claim should not be outweighed by the right to free speech?

The popular catchphrase of free speech defenders is a quote attributed to [French writer] Voltaire: *"I disapprove of what you say, but I will defend to the death your right to say it."* Civil libertarians often defend and support the notion that the right to freely express offensive opinions is a bedrock human right that should not be abridged except under very narrow circumstances—typically for hate speech that directly incites violence against a person or group of persons. However, I support broader prosecution of hate speech—defined here as speech that disparages a person or class of persons based on an immutable characteristic (colour, race, origin, gender, sexual orientation, disability, and age), or their occupation, family or marital status, and religion or lack of religion. Proscribing hate speech more broadly would, I believe, foster a more inclusive, tolerant, and safer society.

The Criminalization of Hate Speech

Many western countries already do criminalize hate speech in a more encompassing way, although enforcement is often weak and spotty. A typical example is Canada, where it is illegal to "expose a person or persons to hatred or contempt . . . on the basis of a prohibited ground of discrimination" (Canadian Human Rights Act) and to "wilfully promote hatred against any identifiable group" (Criminal Code of Canada). The United States, however, stands almost alone in its veneration of free speech at almost any cost. The U.S. Supreme Court insists that the First Amendment protects hate speech unless it constitutes a "true threat" or will incite imminent lawless action.

But societies should take action against hate speech without requiring that a few specific words by themselves must directly and immediately incite violence, or be likely to. That sets a very high bar and is difficult to prove. It also allows purveyors of hate to evade responsibility simply by not making explicit calls for violence. Further, our new digital world raises the stakes—the Internet has spawned a proliferation of hate speech along with useful information such as bomb-making instructions or the home addresses of abortion providers. This has enabled others to commit violence long after the words were first published.

Violent acts of hate are generally preceded by hate speech that is expressed publicly and repeatedly for years, including by public figures, journalists, leading activists, and even the state. Some examples include Anders Behring Breivik's terrorist acts in Norway (June 2011), the assassination of Kansas abortion provider Dr. George Tiller (May 2009) and other abortion providers in the 1990s, the Rwandan genocide against the Tutsis (1994), the ethnic cleansing of Bosnian Muslims in Bosnia-Herzegovina (1992–1995), and the Nazi Holocaust.

Culpability for Violent Crimes

Courts of law should be able to look at broader patterns of hate speech in the culture to determine whether a hateful atmosphere inspired or contributed to violence, or would likely lead to future violence. When hate speech is relatively widespread and acceptable (such as against Muslims or abortion providers), it's not difficult to see the main precursor to violence—an escalation of negative behaviour or rhetoric against the person or group. Dr. George Tiller endured a previous assassination attempt and a decades-long campaign of persecution waged by the anti-abortion movement, which worsened over time, especially in the last year or two of the doctor's life. Anders Behring Breivik had actively opposed multiculturalism for years and had immersed himself in Christian Right propaganda about the supposed threat of Muslim immigration to Europe, a view popularized only in recent years by a growing army of anti-Muslim bloggers and right-wing journalists.

As these examples illustrate, we can often pinpoint the main purveyors of hate speech that lead to violent crimes. In the Norway shootings, the killer Breivik relied heavily on writings from Peder Jensen ("Fjordman"), Pamela Geller, Robert Spencer, Mark Steyn, [the websites] *Jihad Watch, Islam Watch, FrontPage Magazine,* and others. Such individuals and groups should be charged with incitement to hatred and violence. Similar culpability for the assassination of Dr. George Tiller should rest on the shoulders of the extremist anti-abortion group Operation Rescue and Fox News commentator Bill O'Reilly.

In general, anyone spewing hate to an audience, especially on a repeated basis, could be held criminally responsible. This would include politicians, journalists, organizational leaders and speakers, celebrities, bloggers and hosts of online forums, and radical groups that target certain categories of people. We also need to hold people in accountable positions to a higher standard, such as government employees and contractors, ordained religious leaders, CEOs [chief executive officers], and the like.

Criteria by which to assign culpability could include a speaker's past record of prior hate speech against a particular person or group, how widely and frequently the views were disseminated, and the specific content and framing of their views. In cases where violence has already occurred, judges could determine how likely it was that the violent perpetrators had been exposed to someone's specific hate speech, and hand down harsher sentences accordingly.

The Harms of Hate Speech

The apparent assumption of free speech defenders is that offensive speech is essentially harmless—that is, just words with no demonstrable link to consequences. But questioning whether speech can really incite someone to bad behaviour seems irresponsibly obtuse. Obviously, words have consequences and frequently inspire actions. A primary purpose of language is to communicate with others in order to influence them. If that weren't so, there would be no multi-billion dollar advertising industry, no campaigns for political office, no motivational speakers or books, no citizen-led petitions, no public service announcements, and no church sermons, along with a myriad of other proven examples where speech leads others to act.

The majority of hate speech is targeted towards gays, women, ethnic groups, and religious minorities. It's no coincidence that straight white men are generally the most ardent defenders of near-absolute free speech, because it's very easy to defend hate speech when it doesn't hurt you personally. But hate speech is destructive to the community at large because it is divisive and promotes intolerance and discrimination. It sets the stage for violence by those who take the speaker's message to heart, because it creates an atmosphere of perceived acceptance and impunity for their actions. Left unchecked, it can lead to war and genocide, especially when the state engages in hate speech, such as in Nazi Germany.

Hate speech also has serious effects on its targets. Enduring hatred over many years or a lifetime will take a toll on most people. It can limit their opportunities, push them into poverty, isolate them socially, lead to depression or dysfunction, increase the risk of conflict with authority or police, and endanger their physical health or safety. In 1990, the Canadian Supreme Court stated that hate speech can cause "loss of self-esteem, feelings of anger and outrage and strong pressure to renounce cultural differences that mark them as distinct." The court agreed that "hate propaganda can operate to convince listeners . . . that members of certain racial or religious groups are inferior," which can increase "acts of discrimination, including the denial of equal opportunity in the provision of goods, services and facilities, and even incidents of violence."

In democratic societies that stand for equality and freedom—often with taxpayer-funded programs that promote those values by assisting vulnerable groups—it makes no sense to tolerate hate speech that actively works to oppose those values. Further, hate speech violates the spirit of human rights codes and laws, diminishing their purpose and effect. A society that allows hate speech is a society that tolerates prejudice at every level—politically, economically, and socially—and pays the consequences through increased discrimination and violence.

Objections from Hate Speech Defenders

The most popular solution to the problem of hate speech is "more free speech." This seems to make sense on the surface, and sometimes works well in practice. For example, there are many outspoken atheists who do a good job of publicly defending themselves and their fellow atheists from the prejudice and hatred too often expressed by religious people. But even if the targets of hatred can ably defend themselves from verbal violence, why should they have to? Why should a democratic society privilege the right to free speech over the well-being and privacy of those with less privilege?

Most vulnerable groups, however, do not have a level playing field on which to respond to hate speech against them. They are often outnumbered, out-resourced, and out-funded by the haters, simply because of their disadvantaged position in society. Sexism and racism are still thriving in the 21st century, which means women and most minority groups have a harder time getting published and heard and taken seriously in mainstream society. Which brings us full circle—perhaps one of the reasons sexism and racism are still so prevalent in modern society is because free speech is exercised largely by the privileged at the expense of the unprivileged.

A common objection to prosecuting hate speech is that it might endanger speech that *counters* hate speech. For example, a critique may repeat the offending words and discuss their import, or it may subvert the hate message in a subtle or creative way that could be misunderstood by some. But context is every-thing when determining whether speech is actually hateful or not, so this objection seems nonsensical. Any reasonable judge should be able to discern the difference in intent or effect behind a hateful message and the speech that critiques it.

Another objection is that prosecuting hate speech removes accountability from those who actually commit the violence, turning violent perpetrators into victims of hate speech. But no-one is suggesting that hate speech causes people to act against their will or takes away their personal responsibility. Typically, hate speech creates an environment in which a person who is already sympathetic to the views of the speaker feels validated and encouraged to take action, with a reduced fear of punitive consequences and even anticipation of praise and support from the in-group that shares their views. Nothing prevents a hate-inspired murderer from being prosecuted in the same way as any other violent murderer—in fact, many countries mete out harsher penalties for hate-motivated crimes. But those who in-spired the murderer should also be prosecuted separately under hate speech laws.

Existing Restrictions on Free Speech

Many people seem to treat freedom of expression as an almost sacred, inviolable right, but this is far from the reality. In consti-tutional democracies, free speech is already justifiably restricted in a multitude of ways by law or policy, even in the United States. The quintessential example of prohibited speech is falsely shout-ing "Fire!" in a crowded theatre. Besides hate speech itself, some other generally accepted prohibitions of speech include:

- Sedition (advocating force as a way to change the government)
- Threats
- Defamation (libel and slander)
- False or misleading advertising

- Buffer zones around abortion clinics that prevent anti-abortion protesters from harassing patients and staff
- Quiet zones near hospitals or schools
- Municipal bylaws restricting the location, size, type, content, and display of signs, posters, objects, ads, etc.
- Profanity on public airwaves
- Publication refusal, censorship, and the right to edit enforced by news websites, online forums and blogs, newspapers, magazines, radio, and other media
- Company confidentiality policies (such as employees being prohibited from sharing trade secrets or talking to the media)
- Gag orders or publication bans in contracts, court cases, and settlements

In practice, courts will look at circumstances on a case-by-case basis to see where a balance should be struck between freedom of expression and some other value or right. No single right trumps another in all circumstances, not even the right to life. For example, Canada's constitution allows a fundamental right, such as freedom of expression to be limited to protect someone else's fundamental rights, such as the right to life or liberty—or in the case of abortion, women's right to safely access a necessary medical service, which courts have determined outweighs the protesters' right to protest outside clinics.

Some current legal restrictions on free speech are not on the above list because they are clearly illegitimate. One of those is insulting your country's head of state, currently illegal in at least eight countries, mostly in western Europe. This offence is called "lese-majesty," a holdover from the days when kings were divine. But if political leaders are immune to criticism or ridicule, they have far too much power over the people and the country cannot be a true democracy. In general, the public must be allowed to pass judgment on public figures, because the latter owe their position to public support in the first place, which should not be coerced or bought. For example, public figures in the U.S. are not protected from defamation unless it was done with malice—knowledge of falsehood or reckless disregard for the truth.

Many countries also criminalize blasphemy—the criticism of religious doctrines or practices. But the desire to protect religion from criticism is simply a reflection of the insecurity of believers who doubt their own beliefs. Blasphemy laws have more in common with hate speech actually, because they often result in hateful rhetoric and violent acts against the "blasphemers." Further, many religious people have a tendency to confuse hate speech with dissent, such as Catholics who hurl accusations of "bigotry" when someone criticizes Church policies or dogma. But hate speech is personal—it is directed against *people* based on their identifiable characteristics. Dissent on the other hand is speech against other *opinions, beliefs, or positions.* Dissent is an essential component of a free democracy, and it includes blasphemy. In other words, you should be free to attack Catholic policies that protect abusive priests, but it would be hateful to say that all Catholic priests are pedophiles.

Examples of Anti-Abortion Hate Speech

The history of violence against abortion providers makes a very strong case for prosecution of those who disseminate hate speech against them. Almost all of this violence has occurred in the U.S., which makes a compelling argument for limiting First Amendment protections of hate speech.

On a Sunday morning in May 2009, abortion provider Dr. George Tiller was assassinated while attending church in Wichita, Kansas. The killer, Scott Roeder, had been planning the act for some time and had gleaned information about the doctor's movements from Operation Rescue—an anti-abortion group that Roeder was actively involved in and donated money to. This radical group had moved to Wichita in 2002 for the sole purpose of driving Dr. Tiller out of business, and in the seven years leading up to his murder, Operation Rescue (OR) engaged in a relentless campaign of hate and harassment against him, including aggressive picketing, numerous articles and press releases, baseless criminal charges, frivolous lawsuits, and trumped-up grand juries convened against him. (Dr. Tiller was fully vindicated in every legal battle.)

Two years before the assassination, Roeder posted on OR's blog, urging people to attend Dr. Tiller's church. He himself attended the church a few times, and also participated in OR's pickets outside Dr. Tiller's clinic. Roeder was in regular contact with OR's President, Troy Newman, as well as Senior Policy Advisor Cheryl Sullenger, who was convicted in 1988 of conspiring to bomb a California abortion clinic. When Roeder was arrested, Sullenger's phone number was found on a post-it note on the dash of his car. Sullenger later admitted having several previous conversations with Roeder, in which she gave him information on Dr. Tiller's habits and whereabouts, including his trial dates. In the months before the murder, Roeder had attended at least one court hearing—sitting beside OR's President Troy Newman—to hear Dr. Tiller defend himself against scurrilous charges brought by OR.

The Influence of Others

It's clear that Roeder was not a "lone wolf." Perhaps Roeder did not directly involve anyone else in his plans, but no-one develops their views in a vacuum. Dr. Tiller's murder was the natural culmination of over 20 years of anti-abortion harassment and violence directed at him and his clinic, much of it by Operation Rescue. Roeder had been immersed in OR's violent anti-abortion rhetoric for years, so his beliefs and compulsions were fed by that environment, and thrived on it. Obviously, it played an encouraging role in the violence he committed.

Another key person who helped fuel the fire was Fox TV commentator Bill O'Reilly, who has about 3 million listeners. Between 2005 and 2009, Bill O'Reilly and his guest hosts talked about Dr. Tiller on 29 episodes, including just one month before the assassination. The most common epithet repeated many times by O'Reilly was: "Tiller the Baby Killer." Other comments by O'Reilly included: "[Tiller] destroys fetuses for just about any reason right up until the birth date for $5,000." "He's guilty of 'Nazi stuff.'" "This is the kind of stuff that happened in Mao's China, Hitler's Germany, Stalin's Soviet Union." He "has blood on his hands." He's "a moral equivalent to NAMBLA [North American Man/Boy Love Association] and al-Qaida." He operates a "death mill" and a "business of destruction." "I wouldn't want to be [him] if there is a Judgment Day." Although O'Reilly didn't specifically incite someone to murder Dr. Tiller, he put him in the cross-hairs, providing enough motivation and encouragement for someone to carry out the unspoken deed.

Of course, it wasn't just Dr. Tiller and his clinic that were the targets of ongoing harassment and inflammatory hateful rhetoric. The reign of terror directed at clinics and providers across North America has been going on for 35 years—including 9 previous murders and 20 attempted murders of doctors or clinic staff, hundreds of arsons and bombs and butyric acid attacks, and thousands of death threats, stalking, clinic invasions, vandalism, aggressive pickets, and hate mail. Some shootings in the early 1990s were directly preceded by "Wanted Posters" put out by anti-abortion groups on the doctors, complete with their home and clinic addresses and often their photographs. Doctors David Gunn and John Britton were murdered by anti-abortion extremists and had been featured on wanted posters, along with George Tiller, who was shot and wounded in 1993. (The murder of a fourth doctor on a wanted poster, George Patterson, could not be conclusively linked to an anti-abortion extremist.) The posters were deemed by a federal court in 2002 to be a "true threat" under the FACE [Fredom of Access to Clinic Entrances] Act, federal legislation that protects clinics from violence. Noting that the posters had preceded the murders, the court said it was the "use of the 'wanted'-type format in the context of the poster pattern—poster followed by murder—that constitutes the threats," not the language itself. With this decision, the judges overturned a lower court ruling that had deemed the posters and a related website to be "protected speech" because they did not directly threaten violence.

Weighing Free Speech Against Other Rights

When people and courts defend hate speech against abortion providers as "protected speech," it must be asked: Why are abortion providers required to risk their lives so their persecutors can have free speech rights? Why should doctors constantly have to look over their shoulder in fear, go to work in bullet-proof vests, pay out of pocket for security guards and other expensive safety measures, keep their home address a secret and their curtains permanently drawn shut, and see their children ostracized and bullied at school, just so their persecutors have the right to call them "baby killers"? Why does the right to free speech allow members of this vulnerable minority to be openly defamed and targeted for decades until they're finally assassinated? And why do the families of the slain victims have to suffer in their grief and loss, because free speech was deemed more important than the lives of their loved ones?

The idea that vulnerable persons and groups should have to tolerate hate speech against them in the name of freedom of expression—often over decades or a lifetime—is offensive. We're talking about peoples' lives after all—this is not just a philosophical debate. The right to free speech is a fundamental value, but it should not be allowed to outweigh the basic human rights of other people, especially their right to life.

"The ubiquitous European hate-speech laws represent a clear and present danger to freedom of expression in the Western world."

Censorship as "Tolerance"

Jacob Mchangama

In the following viewpoint, Jacob Mchangama argues that the rise in European laws criminalizing hate speech poses a threat to freedom of expression. Mchangama claims that human-rights agreements adopted by European countries have limited recourse for the protection of free speech. Mchangama contends that history shows why hate-speech laws do not promote tolerance and are dangerous. He concludes that the constitutional protection of hate speech in the United States is a better model and actually leads to more tolerance. Mchangama is director of legal affairs at the Center for Political Studies (CEPOS) in Copenhagen, Denmark, a lecturer on international human-rights law at the University of Copenhagen, and a cofounder of Fri Debat, a Danish-based organization seeking to protect freedom of expression.

As you read, consider the following questions:

1. According to the author, what decision did the European Court of Human Rights make about the protection of hate speech?

Jacob Mchangama, "Censorship as 'Tolerance'," *National Review*, vol. 62, no. 13, July 19, 2010. Copyright © 2010 by National Review. All rights reserved. Reproduced by permission.

2. What convention regarding hate speech was adopted by the United Nations in 1965, according to Mchangama?
3. What is the effect of freedom of expression on hatred, propaganda, and racism, according to the author?

In 1670, the Dutch philosopher Baruch Spinoza wrote an emphatic defense of freedom of thought and speech. Spinoza affirmed that freedom of expression is a universal and inalienable right and concluded: "Hence it is that that authority which is exerted over the mind is characterized as tyrannical." He also argued that freedom of expression is indispensable for peaceful coexistence between members of different faiths and races in a diverse society, holding up as an example 17th-century Amsterdam, "where the fruits of this liberty of thought and opinion are seen in its wonderful increase, and testified to by the admiration of every people. In this most flourishing republic and noble city, men of every nation, and creed, and sect live together in the utmost harmony."

In modern-day Europe, Spinoza's insight has not so much been forgotten as turned on its head. There is a pan-European consensus, fertilized by multiculturalism, that tolerance and peaceful coexistence require the restriction rather than the protection of freedom of speech. This has led to the mushrooming of hate-speech and so-called anti-discrimination laws that criminalize expressions characterized as "hateful" or merely "derogatory" toward members of religious, ethnic, national, or racial groups.

The most prominent victim of hate-speech laws is Dutch politician Geert Wilders, who is currently facing charges of insulting Islam and inciting hatred and discrimination against Muslims; in 2009, he was absurdly denied entry to the United Kingdom on the basis of his views. But the Wilders trial is far from unique. In the U.K., Harry Taylor, an atheist campaigner for "reason and rationality," was sentenced to a six-month suspended prison term and banned from distributing "offensive material." Taylor's crime was leaving satirical caricatures of Jesus, the pope, and Mohammed in a multi-faith prayer room at Liverpool's John Lennon Airport. According to the jury, the caricatures constituted "religiously aggravated intentional harassment, alarm or distress." In Belgium, the admittedly quasi-fascist Flemish-nationalist party Vlaams Blok (now Vlaams Belang) was convicted of racism in 2004. In Denmark, where freedom of speech is often given greater weight than elsewhere in Europe, more than 40 persons have been convicted of hate speech since 2000.

Should European victims of hate-speech laws turn for protection to the plethora of human-rights conventions signed by European states, they will discover that no help is forthcoming. The European Court of Human Rights has decided that hate speech is not protected by the European Convention on Human Rights, and the same court has also sanctioned the seizure and censorship of "blasphemous" films and books that insult religious feelings. It distinguishes between expressions that constitute "gratuitous offence" or aim to "destroy the rights of others" and expressions that "contribute to a question of indisputable public interest"—a hopelessly arbitrary standard that turns the very court that is supposed to safeguard freedom of expression into the ultimate censor.

The EU recently adopted a framework decision obligating all 27 member states to criminalize hate speech. This precludes even a unanimous national parliament from abolishing or easing its hate-speech laws. One might have expected the EU's rights watchdog, the Fundamental Rights Agency, to be up in arms about this development, but think again: The agency "very much welcomes" the framework decision and is actively lobbying for new EU-wide legislation extending hate-speech laws to cover sexual orientation and gender identity.

Human-rights agencies are sympathetic to hate-speech laws partly because international human-rights conventions at the United Nations were instrumental in globalizing and mainstreaming them. The U.N.'s International Covenant on Civil and Political Rights (ICCPR) recognizes a right to freedom of expression, but it also states that "any advocacy of national, racial or religious hatred that constitutes incitement to discrimination, hostility or violence shall be prohibited by law."

The first working draft, as early as 1947, included only incitement to violence—universally recognized as a permissible ground for restricting freedom of expression—but the Soviet Union, Poland, and France wanted to include incitement to hatred as well. This was met by resistance from most Western states; the U.S. representative, Eleanor Roosevelt, hardly a libertarian, called the prohibition of incitement to hatred "extremely dangerous." The U.K., Sweden, Australia, Denmark, and most other Western democracies opposed the criminalization of free expression, counseling that fanaticism should be countered through open debate instead.

But these objections did not impress the majority of the U.N.'s member states—Saudi Arabia asserted at the time that Western "confidence in human intelligence was perhaps a little excessive"—and the "incitement to hatred" language was kept in. So it was that a coalition of totalitarian socialist states and Third World countries, many of them ruled by authoritarians, succeeded in turning a human-rights convention into an instrument of censorship.

But things were to get worse. In 1965, the U.N. adopted the Convention for the Elimination of All Forms of Racial Discrimination (CERD). CERD obliges states to criminalize "all dissemination of ideas based on racial superiority or hatred [and] incitement to racial discrimination." Once again, the West was pitted against socialist states and Third World countries with questionable human-rights records, and once again the West came up short. Thus, in the name of human rights, the state was entrusted with an obligation not only to ensure equal protection before the law but to eliminate racial discrimination as such, even in the private sphere, through criminal law. It is not surprising that such an instrument of oppression should appeal to the totalitarian regimes behind the Iron Curtain, which were already skilled in eliminating "undesirable" views through systematic censorship or, if need be, the gulags.

Despite their initial opposition, most Western states ratified both ICCPR and CERD, and European countries from Austria to Sweden accordingly moved to restrict freedom of expression.

The U.N.'s efforts to eliminate hate speech continue to this day. In 1989, several members of the Committee on the Elimination of Racial Discrimination criticized France for allowing Salman Rushdie's *Satanic Verses* to be published, calling the book an incitement to "racial hatred." None other than the U.N.'s special rapporteur on freedom of expression, supposedly the U.N.'s guardian of free speech, publicly condemned both the Mohammed cartoons and Geert Wilders's film *Fitna*. For more than ten years, the Islamic states of the OIC have pushed for criminalizing so-called defamation of religion; their most recent effort concerned a convention to target "cybercrime," including offensive online content. Why has the OIC targeted cybercrime? Because the European states criminalized online hate speech in 2003, and the OIC expects it will be difficult for Europeans to resist its agenda without appearing hypocritical (not to mention Islamophobic). Hate-speech laws have also spread beyond Europe to Canada, New Zealand, and Australia. This leaves the U.S. as the sole Western country with sufficient confidence in reason to let its citizens express themselves freely.

The ubiquitous European hate-speech laws represent a clear and present danger to freedom of expression in the Western world. Not only do they interfere with the basic right of the individual to speak his or her mind even if it causes offense, they are inherently arbitrary and prone to abuse. The determination of which expressions are "hateful" or "derogatory" is highly subjective; the atheist and the fervent believer are unlikely to agree on where the limits of religious satire should be drawn. And in an era of identity politics, when people are encouraged to think

The Origin of Hate-Speech Laws

The origin of hate-speech laws has been largely forgotten. The divergence between the United States and European countries is of comparatively recent origin. In fact, the United States and the vast majority of European (and Western) states were originally opposed to the internationalization of hate-speech laws. European states and the U.S. shared the view that human rights should protect rather than limit freedom of expression.

Rather, the introduction of hate-speech prohibitions into international law was championed in its heyday by the Soviet Union and allies. Their motive was readily apparent. The communist countries sought to exploit such laws to limit free speech.

As Americans, Europeans and others contemplate the dividing line emerging on the extent to which free speech should be limited to criminalize the "defamation of religions" and "Islamophobia," launched by the member states of the Organization of the Islamic Conference (OIC) since 1999, they should bear this forgotten history in mind. However well-intended—and its initial proponents were anything but well-intended—the Western acceptance of hate-speech laws severely limits the ability of liberal democracies to counter attempts to broaden the scope of hate-speech laws under international human rights law, with potentially devastating consequences for the preservation of free speech.

Jacob Mchangama, Policy Review,
December 1, 2011.

of themselves primarily as members of racial, religious, or ethnic groups with special rights rather than as individual citizens with equal rights before the law, "racism" and "hatred" have become very broad concepts indeed.

Moreover, the question of which groups get hate-crime protections depends on political favor. During the Cold War, the gravest danger to the West, indeed the world, stemmed not from the resurrection of racist fascism but from totalitarian socialism. Yet in 1973, a leading Danish socialist was free to declare that "in order for the workers to live they must kill the capitalists. In order for the working class to seize power, it must send the bourgeoisie to its death." Today, Communism and doctrinaire socialism are almost dead in most European states. But the demise of Communism was not achieved by criminalizing this dangerous ideology; it was achieved by, among other things, a vigorous war of ideas that convinced most people that Communism is not only unworkable, but deadly in the extreme.

The Holocaust was still fresh in the minds of those who drafted the hate-speech-related U.N. conventions during the 1950s and '60s, and fresh memories of Nazi atrocities helped them to get those conventions passed. A lax attitude to Nazi propaganda, their argument went, had helped pave the way for Nazi rule and the annihilation of millions of Jews. But justifying hate-speech laws with reference to the Holocaust ignores some crucial points. Contrary to common perceptions, Weimar Germany was *not* indifferent to Nazi propaganda; several Nazis were convicted for anti-Semitic outbursts. One of the most vicious Jew-baiters of the era was Julius Streicher, who edited the Nazi newspaper *Der Stürmer*; he was twice convicted of causing "offenses against religion" with his virulently anti-Semitic speeches and writings. Hitler himself was prohibited from speaking publicly in several German jurisdictions in 1925. None of this prevented Streicher from increasing the circulation of *Der Stürmer*, or Hitler from assuming power. The trials and bans merely gave them publicity, with Streicher and Hitler cunningly casting themselves as victims.

Perhaps even more important, when the Nazis swept to power in 1933, they abolished freedom of expression. Nazi propaganda became official truth that could not be opposed, ridiculed, or challenged with dissenting views or new information. Such a monopoly on "truth" is impossible in a society with unfettered freedom of expression, where all information and viewpoints are subject to intense public debate. While Germans were being brainwashed into hating Jews and acquiescing to the Holocaust, their Lutheran brethren to the north in Denmark—which maintained a free press until it was occupied in 1940—saved most of their country's Jews from extermination.

By empowering an active civil society, freedom of expression can thus be said to include its own safety valve against hatred, propaganda, and racism. There is no clear evidence that hate-speech laws foster a higher degree of racial and religious tolerance or help eradicate racism, and it is in any case both condescending and oppressive for the government to presume it knows which views and information its citizens can be trusted to express. Allowing the unquestionably racist and bigoted to speak their minds does not imply official endorsement of their views, just as declining to criminalize adultery does not imply state endorsement. Racism, religious hatred, and homophobia can and must be combated through an open and unfettered debate. When confronted with genuine hatred, it is perfectly possible—and morally imperative—to heed Holocaust survivor Elie Wiesel's warning that "indifference is not an option" without resorting to coercion and thought control.

In the United States, the First Amendment prohibits hate-speech laws. This has been compatible with, and has plausibly contributed to, the decline of racism. The Ku Klux Klan is no longer a dominant force in southern politics. In 1958, 4 percent of Americans approved of interracial marriage; in 2007, 77 percent did. A Pew study in 2010 showed that large majorities of blacks and whites think their values have become more similar during the past ten years, and that more black Americans blame personal behavior for "blacks who don't get ahead" than blame racism.

When it comes to religious tolerance, the U.S. also stands out. According to a 2010 poll in the *Financial Times*, a full 70 percent of the French and 57 percent of Britons support banning the burqa, compared with only 33 percent of Americans. This American tolerance is hardly born out of sympathy for the ideology the burqa represents, which is responsible for many dead American soldiers in Afghanistan. Rather, Americans hold that the dangers of allowing the state to regulate religious expression greatly outweigh its uncertain benefits.

While perhaps not perfect, the American approach is a vindication of Spinoza's belief in freedom of expression as the oxygen of a diverse society. The European commitment to hate-speech laws, on the other hand, is impossible to reconcile with the Enlightenment values that most Europeans would like to think their societies are committed to.

"Corporations are associations of
individuals, and individuals do not
lose their First Amendment rights
simply because they decide to join with
other individuals under a particular
organizational form."

Citizens United and the Battle for Free Speech in America

Steve Simpson

*In the following viewpoint, Steve Simpson argues that the US Su-
preme Court's 2010 decision in* Citizens United v. Federal Election
Commission *correctly recognized that freedom of speech under
the First Amendment protects individual speech, whether speaking alone or as a member of a larger group such as a corporation.
Simpson claims that opposition to corporate spending in elections
is politically motivated and involves endorsing an incorrect view of
the First Amendment. Simpson is a senior attorney at the Institute
for Justice, a libertarian public interest law firm.*

As you read, consider the following questions:

1. According to Simpson, what is the instrumentalist view of
   the First Amendment?

Steve Simpson, "*Citizens United* and the Battle for Free Speech in America," *Objective Standard*, vol. 5, no. 1, Spring 2010. Copyright © 2010 by Objective Standard. All rights reserved. Reproduced by permission.

2. What speech by the nonprofit organization Citizens United was at issue in its 2010 US Supreme Court case, according to the author?
3. What two previous cases does Simpson cite in support of his claim that the Supreme Court has overturned precedent before the *Citizens United* decision?

The Supreme Court's decision in *Citizens United v. FEC* is one of the most important First Amendment decisions in a generation and one of the most controversial. In it, the Supreme Court struck down a law that banned corporations from spending their own money on speech that advocated the election or defeat of candidates. In the process, the Court overturned portions of *McConnell v. FEC*, a case in which the Supreme Court, a mere six years ago, upheld McCain-Feingold, one of the most sweeping restrictions on campaign speech in history.

In many ways, *Citizens United* is a ringing endorsement of First Amendment rights, and it is certainly cause for optimism about the future of free speech. But the divisions on the Supreme Court over the case and the reactions from Democrats in Congress, the media, and the left in general indicate that *Citizens United* will not be the last word on the matter.

In this respect, the controversy is not surprising: *Citizens United* dealt a serious blow to the further growth of campaign finance laws, supporters of which are determined and outspoken. But the controversy *is* shocking from the standpoint of the law at issue: It prevented a nonprofit group from distributing a film that criticized a candidate, Hillary Clinton, during her run for the presidency in 2008. During oral arguments in the case, the government admitted campaign finance laws could be applied to prevent corporations from publishing and distributing not only films but also *books* that said the wrong things during election cycles.

Banning films and *books*?

The First Amendment states: "Congress shall make no law . . . abridging the freedom of speech, or of the press." Those simple and elegant words would seem to leave no room for a law, passed by Congress, that prevents corporations from spending money to distribute films and books. So, how did we get here?

The answer is that as important as the First Amendment is to America, few Americans have grasped its actual meaning. The amendment properly protects each individual's inviolable right to freedom of speech—regardless of whether anyone's exercise of that right serves a "social purpose." But over time, and especially in the 20th century, the First Amendment came to be viewed by most intellectuals, and by the Supreme Court, in almost exclusively *instrumentalist* terms.[1] Its primary purpose, on the instrumentalist view, is to facilitate the collective "search for truth" allegedly necessary to support "representative self government."[2] In other words, freedom of speech serves not the goals of individuals but those of "society."

Intellectuals, courts, and commentators have debated which particular "social goals" the First Amendment should serve, but few in the 20th century have disagreed that the First Amendment's purpose is primarily instrumental. Seen this way, the First Amendment is effectively a blank slate. And in the early and mid-20th century, so-called "progressives" were happy to write their goals onto it.

Led by intellectuals such as John Dewey and Herbert Croly, the progressives actively opposed the limited, constitutional government established by America's founders.[3] Progressives held that the individual's highest moral purpose is to serve the "greater good" of society. They opposed private property and capitalism, sought to redistribute wealth, and believed that inequalities among citizens justified overriding constitutional limits on government action.[4] Because businesses and the wealthy often lobbied and campaigned against the progressives' efforts, the progressives championed early restrictions on lobbying and campaign spending.

Speech, they said, should be protected only to the extent that it serves the "public interest"—which, in their conception, did not include the interests of businesses and the wealthy.[5] The progressives pejoratively dubbed the interests of businesses and the wealthy "special interests"—interests contrary to the "public interest"—and held that the First Amendment did not protect speech in the service of such interests.[6]

In the modern era, the progressive who most influenced campaign finance laws was John Gardner, the founder of Common Cause.[7] Gardner shared the early progressives' disdain for "special interests," which he believed were thwarting the progressives' agenda by using money to influence the political process. "All citizens should have equal access to decision-making processes of government, but money makes some citizens more equal than others,"[8] Gardner argued. "It isn't just that money talks. It talks louder and longer and drowns out the citizen's hoarse whisper."[9] Gardner and Common Cause were instrumental in crafting and passing the first modern campaign finance reform law in the early 1970s,[10] which set the tone for much of what would follow.

So-called progressives today employ the language established by Gardner, claiming that those who can afford to spend more money to influence the course of government—by, for instance, convincing voters to support or oppose certain politicians—are "more equal" than others. To reduce that inequality, they insist, the government must restrict spending that produces unequal speech. As law professor Owen Fiss puts it, the government "may even have to *silence* the voices of some in order to hear the voices of others. Sometimes there is simply no other way."[11]

This egalitarian view of speech is patently contrary to the First Amendment's protection of the individual's right to *freedom* of speech. Egalitarians ignore the obvious fact that individuals are necessarily *unequal*: Some have more money than others, some are more articulate than others, some are louder and more persistent than others (among countless other differences). If people are left free to speak as they wish—and to pay for the means to do so—some individuals and groups will have a greater impact on elections and thus the policies and actions of government than others. In short, freedom of speech and equality of speech are opposites.

This is the battle at the heart of campaign finance laws. On one side is the view, held (albeit imperfectly) by most challengers of such laws, that the First Amendment protects an individual right to freedom of speech. On the other is the view, held by advocates of campaign finance laws, that the First Amendment protects speech only insofar as it serves, or at least does not thwart, equality of influence over the political process. In the middle is the Supreme Court, which has wavered between these poles, but, unfortunately, has all too often sided with the egalitarians.

The Supreme Court's decision in *Citizens United*, the latest skirmish in this battle, was a substantial victory for the individual rights interpretation of the First Amendment. To understand the significance of this ruling, we must begin by surveying the most relevant history of campaign finance laws. Then we will turn to the *Citizens United* decision itself, the controversy it ignited, and what the Court's ruling means for freedom of speech and the future.

Compromising Freedom of Speech: *Buckley v. Valeo*

The federal government has intermittently regulated various aspects of campaign financing since the early 20th century. Dissatisfied with this patchwork of laws, Congress, in the early 1970s, sought to establish a comprehensive regulatory scheme for all aspects of campaign financing. The result was the Federal Election Campaign Act (FECA), which was first passed in 1971 and substantially revised and strengthened following the Watergate scandals.[12] Like most campaign finance laws, although FECA was very complex, its basic structure was relatively simple. It regulated the money going into campaigns (contributions); it regulated the money coming out of campaigns (expenditures);

and it required all of this to be reported to the government (disclosure).[13] Recognizing that individuals and groups could benefit candidates indirectly, the drafters of FECA extended its reach to so-called "independent expenditures," which are amounts spent by people on their own, independent of a candidate, to promote him or attack his opponent.[14]

Leaving aside the philosophical premises on which the law was based, FECA posed an immediate practical problem. How do you control the money going into campaigns?

Consider the seemingly simple matter of limiting the contributions individuals make to candidates. FECA allows individuals to contribute no more than $2,400 per year to a given candidate. But what counts as a contribution? Obviously, direct monetary donations count, but what about gifts of goods or services? If cash counts as a contribution, then something cash can buy—office equipment, computers, consulting services, or advertising—must count as well, otherwise donors could easily skirt the laws by donating such goods. If people are prevented from helping candidates they support in one way, they will try others.

Consequently, once enacted, laws such as FECA, which aim to regulate financial support for political campaigns, must continually expand as individuals inevitably find ways around them. Faced with a ban on large direct contributions to candidates, individuals will donate money to political parties. Cut off that option, and they will spend their money on their own speech—perhaps purchasing television or radio ads—that supports the candidate. Prevent them from buying broadcast ads, and they will purchase print ads. Block that avenue, and they will use direct mail, the Internet, or some other means. This is the very phenomenon that led the drafters of FECA to include a restriction on independent expenditures: They anticipated people's efforts to skirt the spirit of the law by circumventing the letter of the law.

Free-market thinkers have long understood that laws expand in this manner. Regulation begets regulation, either because it creates dislocations in the marketplace that need to be remedied by more regulation or because the subjects of the regulation find ways around the law. Inevitably, the regulators react by closing the loopholes.

Thus, given the existence of campaign finance laws, we have two alternatives: Allow the laws to expand inexorably until they regulate everything that could benefit a candidate or influence an election, or eliminate the laws entirely.

In 1976, faced with these alternatives, the Supreme Court chose a third option: compromise.

The case was *Buckley v. Valeo*,[15] the first modern campaign finance case and the one that established the constitutional framework within which all campaign finance cases are analyzed to this day. The challengers in *Buckley* contended that FECA's limits on contributions and expenditures violated the First Amendment. They reasoned, quite sensibly, that to speak to a large audience requires the expenditure of large amounts of money. That money must come from somewhere. Any limit on the source of those funds or on the ability to spend them will necessarily limit the speech that the providers of those funds aim to produce.[16]

The Supreme Court accepted half of this argument, striking down limits on expenditures but upholding limits on contributions. Expenditure limits, the Court reasoned, were tantamount to telling someone he could drive as far as he wanted, as long as he did so on one tank of gasoline.[17] Such limits restricted the overall *amount* of speech a candidate could produce, and were thus direct infringements on his freedom of speech.[18]

Contribution limits were a different matter, however. A limit on contributions, according to the Court, did not significantly restrict speech because the speaker could simply raise funds from a larger number of contributors. Although this obviously limited the amounts that individual contributors could donate to a candidate, that was not, as the Court saw it, a significant infringement of First Amendment rights because the contributor was not attempting to speak himself; rather, he was funding the *candidate's* speech, and the candidate remained free to speak.[19]

Moreover, according to the Court, the government had presented a very good reason to limit contributions: the prevention of quid pro quo corruption. If donors were permitted to give large amounts of money to candidates, the reasoning went, candidates might be tempted to provide special favors in return. And even if no such corruption actually occurred, large contributions to candidates might *appear* corrupt to the public.[20] For the Court, both of these rationales were compelling enough to justify what it viewed as a minor infringement on the freedom of speech.

As for FECA's limits on independent expenditures—money individuals spent on their own speech advocating the election or defeat of candidates—the government presented two arguments. First, the government claimed that independent expenditures can lead to quid pro quo corruption just as direct contributions can. For example, if a person buys an advertisement supporting a candidate, it can certainly benefit the candidate in a way that might lead to reciprocation. Second, echoing the progressives, the government argued that limiting independent spending would make elections more "democratic," by equalizing all voices.[21]

The problem for the government, however, was that the Court saw its position as a direct attack on political speech and the rights of citizens to advocate the election or defeat of candidates. Despite the *Buckley* Court's support for limits on contributions, it was unwilling to uphold a law that so clearly and directly prohibited political speech.[22] The Court rejected both of the government's rationales for limiting independent expenditures and struck down these limits.

Regarding the potential for quid pro quo corruption, the Court held that independent expenditures were less likely to lead to corruption, because, under the law, such expenditures had to be truly *independent*—that is, they could not be coordinated with a candidate's campaign. Thus, according to the Court, the benefits to candidates from independent expenditures would be substantially attenuated.[23] As for the egalitarian "fairness" rationale, the Court, in what has become one of its most oft-cited passages, said,

The concept that government may restrict the speech of some elements of our society in order to enhance the relative voice of others is wholly foreign to the First Amendment, which was designed to secure the widest possible distribution of information from diverse and antagonistic sources and to assure the interchange of ideas for the bringing about of social changes desired by the people.[24]

Like so much of the *Buckley* decision, this statement was both promising and frustrating. On this view of the First Amendment, freedom of speech is protected not as an inalienable right of the individual, but as a means to serve a broader "public good"— "the bringing about of social changes desired by the people." Thus, although the Court made the right decision, it did so for the wrong reason.

Despite some high points, the Court's decision in *Buckley* entailed flawed premises and compromised principles that would lead to further infringements on the freedom of speech. Three aspects of the ruling guaranteed this: First, the Court's distinction between contributions and independent expenditures was impossible to maintain over the long term because both can benefit candidates and thus arguably lead to a quid pro quo. Second, although the Court rejected the egalitarian rationale for campaign finance restrictions, the rationale it accepted—the possibility of quid pro quo—was vague. Third, the Court's instrumentalist interpretation of the First Amendment left room for restrictions where speech was believed not to further the "public interest." This was a recipe for disaster.

The *Wall Street Journal* presciently described *Buckley* as having created a "half-dead monster" that is "awfully hard to kill, and the more you wound it, the more havoc it will wreak."[25] To see how this monster terrorized free speech for years to come, we need to work in one more piece of the campaign finance puzzle: the treatment of corporate speech.

Silencing Corporate Speech

Since the early 20th century, federal law has severely restricted corporate spending on political speech, first banning direct corporate contributions to candidates and then banning corporate independent expenditures for electoral advocacy. Supporters of the bans have argued both that corporations are artificial persons without First Amendment rights, and that the bans are necessary to promote equality of influence in elections.[26] Another motivation for such bans, however, is the supporters' desire to silence those with whom they disagree.

For example, the first federal ban on corporate political contributions was the Tillman Act of 1907, named after its chief supporter, segregationist Ben Tillman. Tillman, a Democrat, despised Republican Teddy Roosevelt, who had received a great deal of corporate support during his run for the presidency in 1904.[27] And corporations had opposed Tillman's segregationist policies, which required them to pay for two sets of railcars, drinking fountains, and bathrooms and prevented them from using inexpensive black labor that Tillman wanted to keep out of the labor force.[28]

For more than half a century, the Tillman Act and other such laws (both federal and state) treated corporations differently from individuals, allowing individuals to contribute to candidates and spend money on independent electoral advocacy but banning corporations from doing so. In the 1970s, Congress incorporated these bans into FECA. But it was not until 1990, in *Austin v. Michigan Chamber of Commerce*, that the Supreme Court directly considered whether the government may ban corporations from spending money on their own independent speech about candidates during elections.[29]

At issue in *Austin* was a Michigan law that, like federal law, prohibited corporations from making independent expenditures.

The law prevented the Michigan Chamber of Commerce, a corporation, from publishing an ad in a local newspaper that supported a candidate for the State House of Representatives. Relying on *Buckley*, the Court of Appeals struck down the law as a violation of the First Amendment.[30] When the case reached the Supreme Court, it seemed a sure win for the Chamber of Commerce. Under what possible rationale could the state prevent a corporation from doing what *Buckley* held individuals had a right to do—spend their own money on their own political speech? But the majority in *Austin* found a rationale: the same rationale on which the Court relied in *Buckley* to uphold contribution limits: the possibility of "corruption."

In *Buckley*, the Court had defined the corruption in question as the political quid pro quo—an exchange of campaign contributions for political favors. It concluded that avoiding even the "appearance" of such exchanges was sufficient grounds for limiting contributions.[31] But the Court never defined the corruption it had in mind any more clearly than this. Corruption, according to the Court, was something less than bribery but more than the effort to influence the actions or judgment of politicians.[32] The Court recognized that in a representative form of government, constituents must be permitted to influence politicians' judgment and their actions, but it felt that at some point that influence went "too far." Thus, small contributions would be permissible but not large ones. John Doe would be free to send up to $2,400 to his candidate of choice, but Steve Forbes would not be permitted to bankroll Jack Kemp's run for president. George Soros, however, would be free to spend millions on independent ads supporting his favorite candidate.

The Supreme Court's notion of "corruption" provided no clear, principled reason for why some of these things were permissible and others were not. The so-called progressives were only too happy to exploit this weakness.

Progressives had always believed that any effort by "special interests" to influence the views or actions of politicians—

whether through lobbying, campaign contributions, or simply supporting them with independent speech—would lead to unequal influence and was therefore inherently corrupt. Although in *Buckley* the Court had rejected the more openly egalitarian rationale for limiting campaign financing, its vague notion of "corruption"—which accepted the progressives' basic premise that something was improper about people spending money to support candidates for office—left the back door open for the egalitarian rationale in the future. In *Austin*, the chickens came home to roost.

Reflecting previous decisions in which the Court had hinted that corporations may be treated differently than individuals, the majority in *Austin* argued that corporations get the benefit of certain "state-created advantages," such as limited liability and perpetual life, and that these advantages "not only allow corporations to play a dominant role in the Nation's economy, but also permit them to use resources amassed in the economic marketplace to obtain an unfair advantage in the political marketplace."[33] On this basis, the Court in *Austin* specified a "new" form of corruption: "the corrosive and distorting effects of immense aggregations of wealth that are accumulated with the help of the corporate form and that have little or no correlation to the public's support for the corporation's political ideas."[34]

The Court noted that in *Buckley* it had rejected limits on independent expenditures, but explained that this was because it had concluded that independent expenditures were *less likely* than direct contributions to cause corruption, not because such expenditures could not in principle create concerns about corruption.[35] In *Austin*, the Court simply expanded its previous notion of corruption from "too much" influence over an officeholder's judgment to "too much" influence over the election process as a whole. As the Court put it in *Austin*, "Corporate wealth can unfairly influence elections when it is deployed in the form of independent expenditures, just as it can when it assumes the guise of political contributions."[36]

In 1973, John Gardner formulated the egalitarian mantra that money made some interests "more equal" than others and threatened to give certain "special interests" disproportionate influence over the political process by "drown[ing] out" the voices of ordinary citizens. Roughly twenty years later, this mantra was substantially accepted by the Supreme Court.

Austin set a precedent that virtually guaranteed the steady growth of campaign finance laws at the expense of political speech. The Supreme Court had held, in essence, that the greater one's resources, the greater the constitutional justification for regulating one's ability to affect politics and the outcome of elections. The protections the Court had extended to political speech in *Buckley* were looking less and less justified every day. If an individual may make only small donations directly to a candidate, and if a corporation may not make any donations or independent expenditures at all, why should individuals be permitted to spend unlimited amounts advocating the election or defeat of a candidate?

Austin also highlighted the tension in another distinction the Supreme Court had created in *Buckley*: "express advocacy" versus "issue advocacy."

A full explanation of why the Court created this distinction in *Buckley* is beyond the scope of this article. Suffice it to say that the Court was attempting to cabin the reach of the very broad and often vague provisions of FECA. In essence, the Court in *Buckley* held that the campaign finance laws could apply only to money spent for speech that advocated the election or defeat of candidates using express terms such as "vote for Smith" or the like. The idea, again, was to balance the alleged need for some limits on campaign financing with the right to freedom of speech. Although the government would be permitted to regulate express advocacy in many circumstances, it was not permitted to regulate so-called "issue advocacy," which was speech that did not use express words such as "vote for" or "vote against."[37]

After *Austin*, this distinction became especially important to corporations, because although *Austin* prohibited them from spending money on express advocacy, it left them free to spend money on issue advocacy.

Predictably, that is what corporations did. Individuals, whether acting independently or organized as corporations, do not stop wanting to affect the outcome of elections or to influence the direction of their government just because five justices on the Supreme Court conclude that they should do so more "fairly." Prevented from running ads that said "vote against Smith," many corporations simply spent their money on ads that said "Smith supports bad policies."

Just as predictably, politicians and others who supported campaign finance laws began to complain. The Supreme Court had said in *Austin* that corporations cannot use their wealth to influence elections, but, according to these complaints, corporations were able to do so after *Austin* by means of issue advocacy rather than express advocacy. This loophole, argued supporters of the laws, enables "special interest" money to corrupt office-holders and tilt the playing field in favor of the wealthy. If we are to eliminate corruption in politics, they concluded, this and other loopholes must be closed.

Twelve years after *Austin*, they got their wish.

McCain-Feingold: Cashing in on *Buckley*'s Compromise

In 2002, Congress passed the Bipartisan Campaign Reform Act, more popularly known as McCain-Feingold.[38] According to Senator John McCain, one of the bill's chief sponsors, the bill was "about curbing the influence of special interests."[39] For many supporters of campaign finance laws, McCain-Feingold was the culmination of decades of work. In *Buckley* the Supreme Court had rejected a central pillar of FECA—its restrictions on both campaign and independent spending. As a result, according to proponents of the laws, "special interests" were still able to funnel unregulated or "soft" money into the campaign finance system. The point of the new law, as McCain put it, was "to stop the use of soft money as a means of buying influence and access with Federal officeholders and candidates."[40] McCain-Feingold accomplished its goal primarily by closing what were seen as two loopholes in the campaign finance laws: First, the ability of individuals to make unlimited contributions to political parties so long as the money was not given directly to candidates; and second, the ability of corporations to spend their money on independent "issue advocacy"—that is, on ads that advocate issues or policies without using words of express advocacy such as "vote for" or "vote against."[41]

McCain-Feingold dealt with the former by creating a series of new limits on contributions to political parties. It dealt with the latter by creating a new category of restricted speech known as "electioneering communications." An electioneering communication is a broadcast communication—such as a television or radio ad—that mentions a candidate within thirty days of a primary or sixty days of a general election.[42] Although issue advocacy does not involve the use of language that expressly advocates the election or defeat of candidates, it does typically refer to candidates by name. Corporations and other groups that had been engaging in issue advocacy also typically used television or radio ads close to an election, because that was the most effective way to reach voters at a time when they were deciding which way to vote. The obvious solution, according to McCain and his allies, was to prevent them from spending money on ads that mentioned a candidate at all. As McCain succinctly put it:

> If you cut off the soft money, you're going to see a lot less [attack advertising]. Prohibit unions and corporations [from spending money on independent ads] and you will see a lot less of that. If you demand full disclosure for those that pay for those ads, you're going to see a lot less of that. . . .[43]

In March 2002, President Bush signed McCain-Feingold into law. It was immediately challenged in court as a violation of the First Amendment. Most observers, including, reportedly, President Bush himself, thought the Supreme Court would strike down the law. In December 2003, however, the Court, in a 5-4 decision, upheld every major provision of the law, including the ban on electioneering communications. . . .

Supporters of campaign finance laws were ecstatic. Their dream of a law that corrected problems they believed had existed since *Buckley* had come true. The decision, *McConnell v. FEC*,[44] was widely regarded at the time to be the most important campaign finance decision since *Buckley*. And, indeed, to uphold a law that regulated political speech more extensively than any law Congress had passed to date, the Court had to break new constitutional ground. It did so primarily by developing a new rationale for upholding campaign finance laws under the First Amendment.

In *Buckley*, the Court held that the only justification for laws limiting campaign financing was the potential for the "corruption" of politicians. In *Austin*, the Court expanded the justification beyond the corruption of candidates to include the "corruption" of the electoral process that allegedly results when corporations are able to spend more on electoral advocacy than others. In *McConnell*, the Court went still further, deciding the government could limit campaign financing to prevent individuals and corporations from circumventing laws that were designed to prevent such corruption.[45]

This was entirely logical given the premises of campaign finance law. *Buckley* implicitly conceded something was wrong with people using money to support candidates or advocate policies. The Court's reasons—inherent in its view of "corruption"— were vague, but there was no mistaking the conclusion that campaign financing is, in some sense, illegitimate. In *Austin*, that implicit premise was made more explicit in the Court's adoption of an egalitarian rationale for limiting corporate spending, which allowed even more limits than *Buckley* had approved. However, those seeking to influence elections were still finding entirely legal ways around the laws. Thus, according to those opposed to such influence, if the goal is to prevent money from infecting politics, the government must be given the constitutional authority to close loopholes as they arise.

Following this logic, the Court in *McConnell* simply observed that many groups were able to use issue advocacy to influence the outcome of elections, and whether or not these groups used words of express advocacy, voters were getting the message. The Court thus concluded that issue advocacy was a "sham"—just another way to achieve the same goals as express advocacy, only less open and honest, and it upheld the electioneering communications ban.[46]

On one level, the implications of the Court's holding in *McConnell* are astounding. Corporations had been expressing themselves through issue advocacy because the Supreme Court had permitted the government to regulate express advocacy, allegedly on the grounds that express advocacy was not protected by the First Amendment but issue advocacy was. In other words, corporations were doing what the Supreme Court had said the First Amendment expressly protected their *right* to do. Yet here was the Supreme Court in *McConnell* holding that the government could now ban a form of issue advocacy—electioneering communications—precisely because corporations were using it in accordance with that right.

On another level, *McConnell's* holding was entirely predictable. As Ayn Rand observed: "In any *conflict* between two men (or two groups) who hold the *same* basic principles, it is the more consistent one who wins."[47] The Court had long accepted the basic principles underlying campaign finance laws. On the *instrumentalist* interpretation of the First Amendment, freedom of speech is not an individual right, but, rather, as Supreme Court Justice Stephen Breyer puts it, a means to "encourage the exchange of information and ideas necessary for citizens them-

The US Supreme Court's View on Speech Restrictions

Premised on mistrust of governmental power, the First Amendment stands against attempts to disfavor certain subjects or viewpoints. Prohibited, too, are restrictions distinguishing among different speakers, allowing speech by some but not others. As instruments to censor, these categories are interrelated: Speech restrictions based on the identity of the speaker are all too often simply a means to control content.

Quite apart from the purpose or effect of regulating content, moreover, the Government may commit a constitutional wrong when by law it identifies certain preferred speakers. By taking the right to speak from some and giving it to others, the Government deprives the disadvantaged person or class of the right to use speech to strive to establish worth, standing, and respect for the speaker's voice. The Government may not by these means deprive the public of the right and privilege to determine for itself what speech and speakers are worthy of consideration. The First Amendment protects speech and speaker, and the ideas that flow from each. . . .

We find no basis for the proposition that, in the context of political speech, the Government may impose restrictions on certain disfavored speakers. Both history and logic lead us to this conclusion.

Anthony Kennedy, Citizens United v. Federal Election Commission, *January 21, 2010.*

selves to shape that public opinion which is the final source of government in a democratic state" and to maintain a government "open to participation . . . by all citizens, without exception."[48] And on the *egalitarian* view of the First Amendment, the state should, quoting Justice Breyer again, "seek to democratize [i.e., equalize] the influence that money can bring to bear upon the electoral process."[49] The only way to equalize people's ability to speak is to outlaw the means by which some can speak more readily than others. That is what the government, with the blessing of the Court, has proceeded to do.

Citizens United: Freeing Speech

By the 2008 elections, the previous three decades of modern campaign finance law had spawned a complex web of statutes, regulations, and court decisions that rival the Internal Revenue Code in their complexity. The Federal Election Commission has produced 568 pages of regulations, 1,278 pages of explanations and justifications for those rules, and 1,771 pages of advisory opinions that offer the agencies' views on particular applications of the law. The laws have created 71 distinct types of regulated entities that are subject to separate rules for 33 different types of political speech. To implement one recent Supreme Court decision that had tried to draw a line between express advocacy and issue advocacy in certain circumstances, the FEC adopted a two-part, eleven-factor balancing test, the outcome of which determined whether one was allowed to speak or faced fines and possibly time in jail.[50]

During the 2008 presidential election cycle, Citizens United, a nonprofit corporation dedicated to "conservative" causes, attempted to navigate this web of regulations and speak its mind about one of the candidates. It produced a one-hour film, *Hillary: The Movie*, which was highly critical of Mrs. Clinton as a person and as a candidate for high office. The group wanted to distribute the film through on-demand cable television during the 2008 primary season. However, the electioneering communications ban covered cable television along with other types of broadcasts, so Citizens United could not distribute its film at any time within thirty days of a primary or sixty days of a general election. And, given the frequency of presidential primaries, it would be prohibited from distributing its film for virtually the entire year preceding the general election. Citizens United sued the FEC, claiming that the law violated its First Amendment right to freedom of speech.[51]

When *Citizens United v. FEC* reached the Supreme Court, most observers thought the Court would rule relatively narrowly. Chief Justice John Roberts was generally regarded as a "judicial minimalist" who placed great importance on precedent and Congress's authority and who favored narrow rulings over broad pronouncements. Justice Samuel Alito, also relatively new to the Court, was a less-known commodity, but both he and Justice Roberts had voted to create a narrow exemption to the electioneering communications ban in an earlier case rather than to rule the entire law unconstitutional. But the Court surprised practically everyone: Its decision went far beyond what anyone had expected early in the case.

Perhaps fed up with the mind-numbing complexity of the campaign finance laws, perhaps concerned by the fact that they were now being used to prevent the distribution of a film, perhaps shocked by the government's admission that the laws could also apply to the publication of books, five justices in *Citizens United* acted to repair some of the damage that had been done to the First Amendment.

Ruling that individuals may not be deprived of freedom of speech simply because they adopt the corporate form, the Court struck down the electioneering communications ban in its entirety. Along with it went the portion of *McConnell* that had upheld the ban as well as the entire *Austin* decision, which had provided the constitutional justification for regulating corporate independent expenditures in the first place. In reversing these cases, the Court effectively tossed out speech-squelching laws that had been on the books in one form or another since 1947.

The Court recognized the stranglehold that campaign finance laws had applied to political speech, likening the byzantine laws to a prior restraint on speech.[52] It said such complex laws, the necessity of hiring lawyers to interpret them, and the lawsuits to which they lead inevitably chill free speech.[53] The Court implicitly criticized its own prior decisions, saying "Courts, too, are bound by the First Amendment" and "must decline to draw, and then redraw constitutional lines" that determine who may speak and who may not.[54] The Court noted that the FEC's "business is to censor speech" and warned against the incremental destruction of speech that results from authorizing bureaucrats to decide how and when we may speak.[55] And it demonstrated that the ban on corporate electoral advocacy would ultimately mean regulation of books, newspapers, the Internet, and *all* forms of expression.[56]

Citizens United is one of the most sweeping endorsements of First Amendment rights and their crucial place in our constitutional republic the Supreme Court has ever issued. Echoing James Madison's view of free speech as "the right of freely examining public characters and measures . . . which has ever been justly deemed, the only effectual guardian of every other right,"[57] the Court said, "Speech is an essential mechanism of democracy, for it is the means to hold officials accountable to the people."[58] "The right of citizens to inquire, to hear, to speak, and to use information to reach consensus is a precondition to enlightened self-government and a necessary means to protect it."[59]

The Court in *Citizens United*, however, understood the freedom of speech to be more than a means to public ends; it saw this freedom also as an *individual right*: "The First Amendment confirms the freedom to think for ourselves"[60] and "it protects speech and speaker, and the ideas that flow from each."[61] If people say things others would rather not hear, said the Court, that is not the government's concern: "it is our law and our tradition that more speech, not less, is the governing rule."[62]

On the core question of whether the ban on corporate spending for independent electoral advocacy violated the First Amendment, *Citizens United* is a model of principled jurisprudence and common sense. The Court recognized that speaking out in today's world often requires large expenditures of money, so a ban on corporate independent expenditures amounts to an outright ban on speech.

> The censorship we now confront is vast in its reach. The Government has muffle[d] the voices that best represent the most significant segments of the economy. And the electorate [has been] deprived of information, knowledge and opinion vital to its function. By suppressing speech of manifold corporations, both for-profit and non-profit, the Government prevents their voices and viewpoints from reaching the public and advising voters on which persons and entities are hostile to their interests.[63]

The Court recognized that corporations are associations of individuals, and individuals do not lose their First Amendment rights simply because they decide to join with other individuals under a particular organizational form, whether corporate or otherwise.[64]

As to the justifications for the law, the Court rejected *Austin's* view that corporations have an unfair advantage in elections as inconsistent not only with *Buckley*, but also with one of the framers' key insights. Special interests—or "factions" in the framers' words—would no doubt form from time to time and try to influence the course of government. But for the Court, as for the founders, limiting freedom of speech would be like eliminating air to prevent fire. Quoting *The Federalist No. 10*, the Court said, "Factions will necessarily form in our Republic, but the remedy of 'destroying the liberty' of some factions is 'worse than the disease.' . . . Factions should be checked by permitting them all to speak . . . and by entrusting the people to judge what is true and what is false."[65]

The Court also rejected the claim that independent expenditures cause corruption. "The fact that speakers may have influence over or access to elected officials does not mean that these officials are corrupt."[66] After all, the Court recognized, representative government necessarily means that citizens are entitled to try to influence what their representatives do: "The fact that a corporation, or any other speaker, is willing to spend money to try to persuade voters presupposes that the people have the ultimate influence over elected officials."[67] Summing up, the Court stated: "If the First Amendment has any force, it prohibits Congress from fining or jailing citizens, or associations of citizens, for simply engaging in political speech."[68]

Citizens United is an astoundingly good decision, especially when compared to the decisions preceding it. It is not just a good campaign finance decision; it is one of the best First Amendment decisions the Supreme Court has ever issued.

But it is not without its flaws.

Most notably, in this regard, the Court maintained the basic framework for analyzing campaign finance laws established in *Buckley*, according to which the government may limit campaign financing, and thus the speech it produces, by showing that its limits serve the purpose of preventing quid pro quo corruption. More fundamentally, by failing to reject the instrumentalist interpretation of the First Ammendment, the Court failed to challenge the idea that the First Amendment means anything other than what it says: "Congress shall make *no* law . . . *abridging* the *freedom* of speech, or of the press" (emphasis added).

Thus, although the Court emphasized, perhaps more than in any other decision, the fact that the First Amendment protects an individual right, the instrumentalist approach to the amendment remains part of the law. Indeed, as indicated by the caustic reaction to this decision from the left, *Citizens United* has not settled the debate over the individualist vs. instrumentalist interpretation.

Critics have called the decision an example of unbridled judicial activism that will corrupt elections and destroy "democracy." According to Democratic Senator Charles Schumer, "The Supreme Court has just predetermined the winners of next November's election. It won't be the Republicans or the Democrats and it won't be the American people; it will be

Corporate America."[69] President Obama, in his State of the Union address, accused the Court of reversing "a century of law that . . . will open the floodgates for special interests—including foreign corporations—to spend without limit in our elections."[70] The *New York Times*—a corporation whose very existence as a source of news explicitly depends on the First Amendment—complained that the decision improperly extended First Amendment rights to corporations.[71] MSNBC commentator Keith Olbermann compared the decision to *Dred Scott*, a case in which the Supreme Court held that an escaped slave must be returned to the slave owner.[72]

What explains this near hysteria over *Citizens United?*

Has the left suddenly become concerned with "judicial activism"? Not likely. The Court has overturned precedent before, most notably in *Brown v. Board of Education*,[73] in which it overturned *Plessy v. Ferguson*'s doctrine of separate but equal, and in *Lawrence v. Texas*,[74] in which it overturned *Bowers v. Hardwick* in the process of striking down antisodomy laws. Somehow, the critics of *Citizens United* have managed to remain silent about these instances of "activism."[75]

Perhaps critics are concerned about extending First Amendment protections to corporations, which are alleged to be only "artificial persons" and mere creatures of the state. However, as the Court itself noted in *Citizens United*, it has treated corporations the same as individuals under the First Amendment for at least half a century. The media, in particular, have benefited from these rulings without ever noticing that the Court was protecting the rights of corporations. And critics of *Citizens United* complain about spending in campaigns regardless of whether it is by corporations, other groups, or individuals.[76]

Clearly, the outrage over *Citizens United* has little to do with the nature of corporations or "judicial activism." Instead, it represents a fundamental philosophical dispute about the nature and meaning of the First Amendment and its role not only in elections but in our entire system of government. So-called

progressives, who are the primary champions of campaign finance laws, oppose individual rights, capitalism, and the constitutional system that protects or makes these values possible; thus
they want to expand the size and scope of government. Freedom
of speech—especially when combined with wealth that enables
people and corporations to speak their minds effectively—stands
in their way.

It is no accident that campaign finance laws often prevent
those most able to oppose the growth of government from
speaking out. Early progressives sought to limit the influence of
corporations because corporations often opposed the progressive agenda of regulations, wealth redistribution, and the like.[77]
John Gardner, the father of the modern campaign finance reform
movement, equated congressional corruption with the failure to
enact such "progressive" policies.[78] And in recent times, many
proponents of McCain-Feingold have expended far more effort
policing "attack ads" than any *quid pro quo* corruption on the
part of politicians.[79]

Citizens United is a truly radical decision, in that it returns to
the constitutional principle that the government must protect and
not violate freedom of speech. Unfortunately, because few people
understand the moral foundation of free speech—namely, the
principle that each individual morally *must*, be left free to speak
his own mind for his own sake because each individual morally
should act on his own judgment for his own sake—freedom of
speech remains not only vulnerable but in severe danger. Until
the First Amendment is interpreted in a manner consistent with
the purpose of government envisioned by the founders—that is,
to protect the rights of individuals to act on their own judgment
regardless of what others think or feel about it—the battle over
free speech will continue.

Notes

Acknowledgment: The author would like to thank Craig Biddle for his helpful edits and
suggestions on this article.

Should Limits Be Placed on Freedom of Expression?

1. Calvin R. Massey, "The Influence of the Foundational Paradigms of Individualism, Pluralism, and Cultural Authoritarianism upon Freedom of Expression," in *Speaking Freely: The Case Against Speech Codes*, edited by Henry Mark Holzer (Studio City, CA: Second Thoughts Books, 1994), pp. 46–60.
2. Massey, "Foundational Paradigms," pp. 46–60.
3. John Samples, *The Fallacy of Campaign Finance Reform* (Chicago: University of Chicago Press, 2006), pp. 43–48; Richard A. Epstein, *How Progressives Rewrote the Constitution* (Washington, D.C.: Cato Institute, 2006), pp. 7–9.
4. Samples, *Fallacy of Reform*, pp. 43–48, 55; Epstein, *How Progressives Rewrote the Constitution*, pp. 7–8.
5. Samples, *Fallacy of Reform*, p. 55; Epstein, How Progressives Rewrote the Constitution, pp. 7–8.
6. Samples, *Fallacy of Reform*, pp. 50, 54–55.
7. Samples, *Fallacy of Reform*, pp. 59–64.
8. John Gardner, *In Common Cause: Citizen Action and How it Works*, quoted in Samples,*Fallacy of Reform*, p. 62.
9. Samples, *Fallacy of Reform*, p. 62.
10. John Gardner: *Uncommon American*, available at http://www.pbs.org/johngardner /chapters/6.html.
11. Owen Fiss, *The Irony of Free Speech* (Cambridge, MA: Harvard University Press, 1996), p. 4 (emphasis added).
12. Anthony Corrado et al., *The New Campaign Finance Sourcebook* (Washington, D.C.: Brookings Institution Press, 2005), pp. 20–22.
13. Corrado et al., *Campaign Finance Sourcebook*, pp. 21–23.
14. Corrado et al., *Campaign Finance Sourcebook*, p. 23.
15. *Buckley v. Valeo*, 424 U.S. 1 (1976) (emphasis added).
16. *Buckley*, 424 U.S. at 11.
17. *Buckley*, 424 U.S. at 19 n. 18.
18. *Buckley*, 424 U.S. at 19.
19. *Buckley*, 424 U.S. at 20–22.
20. *Buckley*, 424 U.S. at 26–29.
21. *Buckley*, 424 U.S. at 48–49.
22. *Buckley*, 424 U.S. at 47–48.
23. *Buckley*, 424 U.S. at 45–47.
24. *Buckley*, 424 U.S. at 48–49.
25. "The Half-Dead Monster," *Wall Street Journal*, February 2, 1976.
26. Samples, *Fallacy of Reform*, p. 45.
27. Bradley A. Smith, *Unfree Speech: The Folly of Campaign Finance Reform* (Princeton: Princeton University Press 2001), p. 23.
28. Bradley Smith, "The Myth of Campaign Finance Reform," *National Affairs*, no. 2, Winter 2010. Like the federal bans on corporate campaign spending, state bans were also motivated in part by a desire to prevent political outcomes corporations supported. See Smith, *Unfree Speech*, p. 23.
29. *Austin v. Michigan Chamber of Commerce*, 494 U.S. 660 (1990).
30. *Austin*, 494 U.S. at 656.
31. *Buckley*, 424 U.S. at 26–27.
32. *Buckley*, 424 U.S. at 27–28. See also *Nixon v. Shrink Mo. Gov't Pac*, 528 U.S. 377, 389 (2000).
33. *Austin*, 494 U.S. at 658 (internal citations and quotation marks omitted).

34. *Austin*, 494 U.S. at 661.
35. *Austin*, 494 U.S. at 659.
36. *Austin*, 494 U.S. at 660.
37. *Buckley*, 424 U.S. at 42–44.
38. Corrado et al., *Campaign Finance Sourcebook*, pp. 37–39.
39. Samples, *Fallacy of Reform*, p. 3.
40. Samples, *Fallacy of Reform*, p. 3.
41. Corrado et al., *Campaign Finance Sourcebook*, pp. 37–39.
42. Corrado et al., *Campaign Finance Sourcebook*, p. 42.
43. Senator John McCain, 107th Cong., 1st Sess., *Congressional Record* (2001), 147:S3116.
44. *McConnell v. FEC*, 540 U.S. 93 (2003).
45. *McConnell v. FEC*, 540 U.S. at 136–137, 143–145.
46. *McConnell v. FEC*, 540 U.S. at 193–194.
47. Ayn Rand, "The Anatomy of Compromise," in *Capitalism: The Unknown Ideal* (New York: Signet, 1967), p. 145.
48. Stephen Breyer, *Active Liberty: Interpreting Our Democratic Constitution* (New York: Alfred A. Knopf, 2005), p. 47 (internal quotation marks omitted).
49. Breyer, *Active Liberty*, p. 47.
50. *Citizens United*, slip op. at 18.
51. *Citizens United*, slip op. at 2–4.
52. *Citizens United*, slip op. at 18.
53. *Citizens United*, slip op. at 7, 19.
54. *Citizens United*, slip op. at 9–10.
55. *Citizens United*, slip op. at 18.
56. *Citizens United*, slip op. at 33, 35–37.
57. James Madison, "Virginia Resolutions Against the Alien and Sedition Acts," (December 21, 1798), reprinted in *James Madison Writings* (Jack N. Rakove, ed., 1999), p. 590.
58. *Citizens United*, slip op. at 23.
59. *Citizens United*, slip op. at 23.
60. *Citizens United*, slip op. at 40.
61. *Citizens United*, slip op. at 23.
62. *Citizens United*, slip op. at 45.
63. *Citizens United*, slip op. at 38 (internal citations and quotation marks omitted).
64. *Citizens United*, slip op. at 25–28.
65. *Citizens United*, slip op. at 39.
66. *Citizens United*, slip op. at 43.
67. *Citizens United*, slip op. at 44.
68. *Citizens United*, slip op. at 33.
69. "GOP Doesn't Run 2010 Census, But Hopes to Count Your Money," *Post Standard* (Syracuse, NY), January 24, 2010, p. A9.
70. President Barack Obama, State of the Union Address, January 27, 2010.
71. "The Court's Blow to Democracy," *New York Times*, January 21, 2010.
72. *Countdown with Keith Olbermann* (MSNBC television broadcast January 21, 2010), available at http://www.msnbc.msn.com/id/3036677/ns/msnbc_tv-countdown_with _keith_olbermann#34984984.
73. *Brown v. Bd. of Education*, 347 U.S. 483 (1952).
74. *Lawrence v. Texas*, 539 U.S. 558 (2003).
75. Indeed, many of *Citizens United*'s harshest critics—including Justice Stevens, who wrote the dissent—have long advocated overturning the portions of *Buckley* that re-

jected limits on independent expenditures. See *Randall v. Sorrell*, 126 S.Ct. 2479, 2506 (2006) (Stevens, J., dissenting). These critics can hardly complain about the majority overturning campaign finance decisions when they wish to do the same to achieve precisely the opposite result.

76. Brief for the Federal Election Commission, p. 43, *SpeechNow.org* v. FEC, No. 09-5342 (D.C. Cir. Dec. 15, 2009).
77. Smith, *Unfree Speech*, p. 23; *Myth of Campaign Finance Reform*.
78. Samples, *Fallacy of Reform*, pp. 62–63.
79. Samples, *Fallacy of Reform*, pp. 3–7, 36.

"*The extraordinary ruling in* Citizens United *is unhinged from traditional American understandings of both the First Amendment and corporations.*"

The First Amendment Does Not Protect Corporate Spending on Political Speech

Jeffrey D. Clements

In the following viewpoint, Jeffrey D. Clements argues that the US Supreme Court erred in finding First Amendment protection for corporate political spending in Citizens United v. Federal Election Commission. *Clements claims that the privileges of corporations have always been and should always be determined by the people, whom he claims are overwhelmingly opposed to unfettered corporate influence in elections. He concludes that a constitutional amendment should be enacted to overturn the* Citizens United *decision. Clements is cofounder and general counsel of Free Speech for People and the author of* Corporations Are Not People.

As you read, consider the following questions:

1. According to the author, which two prior Supreme Court cases were overruled by the Court's decision in *Citizens United?*

2. According to Clements, what entity ranked first in spending for lobbying in the first decade of the twenty-first century?

3. What 1907 law banned corporate political contributions in federal campaigns, according to the author?

The extraordinary response to the *Citizens United* [*v. Federal Election Commission (FEC) (2010)*] decision reflects widespread understanding that the Supreme Court majority's radical interpretation of the First Amendment to hold that the American people and our elected representatives are powerless to regulate corporate political expenditures is fundamentally wrong as a matter of constitutional law, history, and our republican principles of self-government. The revulsion against the majority's action in *Citizens United* cuts across all partisan lines: 81% of Independents, 76% of Republicans, and 85% of Democrats oppose the decision, and 72% of the people support reinstating the very limits that the Court struck down.

In this testimony, I will address the consequences of the pernicious "corporate speech" theory that resulted in the *Citizens United* holding, and the far worse consequences to come. I also hope to show why these consequences are not the result of the limitations or implications of our First Amendment and Bill of Rights, but arise from a new and deeply flawed activism on the bench that the American people and Congress should move promptly to correct.

The Challenge to Corporate Political Expenditure Regulations

Citizens United involved a corporate challenge to the most recent effort to control the corrupting and unfair influence of corporate money in politics: the Bipartisan Campaign Reform Act passed in 2002, frequently called the McCain-Feingold law after its Republican and Democratic Senate sponsors. This law extended pre-existing statutes prohibiting corporations from using corporate funds to advocate voting for or against a candidate for federal office.

Sweeping aside *McConnell v. FEC*, decided only six years ago, and overruling *Austin v. Michigan Chamber of Commerce*, a 1990 case upholding state law restrictions on corporate political expenditures, the Court held that the restrictions on corporate expenditures violated First Amendment protections of free speech. In effect, the majority decision (Justice Anthony Kennedy, joined by Chief Justice John Roberts and Justices Antonin Scalia, Clarence Thomas and Samuel Alito) equates corporations with people for purposes of free speech and campaign expenditures.

The extraordinary ruling in *Citizens United* is unhinged from traditional American understandings of both the First Amendment and corporations. As Justice Stevens' dissent in *Citizens United* makes clear, *Austin, McConnell* and a substantial line of Supreme Court and lower court cases, backed by two centuries of Constitutional jurisprudence, correctly ruled that Congress and the States may regulate corporate political expenditures not because of the type of speech or political goals sought by corporations but because of the very nature of the corporate entity itself. In other words, cases challenging corporate political expenditure regulations are not really about the speech rights of the American people; they are about the power of the American people to regulate corporations and the rules that govern such entities. Justice John Paul Stevens' dissent rightly calls the majority opinion a "radical departure from what has been settled First Amendment law."

The Definition of a Corporation

Remarkably, in a case where the central question is the role and place of corporations in our democracy, Justice Kennedy's opinion does not once define or explain what a corporation is, nor does he even touch upon the legal definition or features of a corporation. Instead, in what Justice Stevens' compelling dissent calls "glittering generalities," the majority opinion focuses on "associations of citizens," "speakers," "voices," and, apparently without irony, a "disadvantaged person or class."

It is a basic and fundamental understanding in the law [according to experts Oscar Handlin and Mary Flug Handlin] that corporations are not "associations of citizens," but are creatures of statute, usually State statute, with characteristics defined by their charters and the state laws that authorize the use of corporate charters. "Those who feel that the essence of the corporation rests in the contract among its members rather than in the government decree . . . fail to distinguish, as the eighteenth century did, between the corporation and the voluntary association."

Corporations cannot exist unless elected representatives choose to enact laws that enable people to organize a corporation and provide the rules of the road for using a corporation. People can start and run businesses without government involvement or permission; people can form advocacy groups, associations, unions, political parties and other groups that exist without the government's authorizing statute. But people, or even "associations of citizens," cannot form or operate a corporation unless the state enacts a law providing authority to form a corporation, and providing the rules of the road that go with use of the corporate form.

The Difference Between Privileges and Rights

Advantages of the corporate form are a privilege provided by government for sound policy reasons. We the people do that through our legislatures because we think, accurately I believe, that such advantages are economically to the advantage of all of us and society over the long haul. Yet corporations, particularly powerful global corporations—and too many judges—confuse these privileges and policies with Constitutional rights.

The Supreme Court used to resist this confusion. As the Court said in *Austin v. Michigan*, one of the cases overruled by *Citizens United*:

State law grants corporations special advantages—such as limited liability, perpetual life, and favorable treatment of the accumulation and distribution of assets. . . . These state-created advantages not only allow corporations to play a dominant role in the Nation's economy, but also permit them to use 'resources amassed in the economic marketplace' to obtain 'an unfair advantage in the political marketplace.'

Similarly, in *McConnell v. FEC*, the Court pointed to "the corrosive and distorting effects of immense aggregations of wealth that are accumulated with the help of the corporate form and that have little or no correlation to the public's support for the corporation's political ideas."

The Spending Impact of the Ruling

What is the likely impact of *Citizens United*'s "radical departure" from this understanding? The data suggest the consequences if the American people do not—or, according to the Court, cannot—control corporate money in politics:

- According to the 2009 Statistical Abstract of the United States, post-tax corporate profits in 2005 were almost $1 trillion.
- During the 2008 election cycle, Fortune 100 companies— the 100 largest corporations—alone had combined revenues of $13.1 trillion and profits of $605 billion.
- In contrast, during the same 2008 cycle, all political parties combined spent $1.5 billion and all of the federal PACs, or political action committees, spent $1.2 billion.

If we take only the profit of the 100 largest corporations alone, those corporations would need less than 2 percent of their $605 billion in profit to make political expenditures that would double all current political spending by all of the parties and all of the federal PACs. Another way to look at it: Assume the 100 largest corporations wished to double—and therefore, swamp—

President [Barack] Obama's 2008 record fundraising effort, much of it from small, individual contributions. That would require shaving a little more than the slightest fraction—1/100—off the top of corporate profits from those 100 corporations.

To suggest that corporations will choose not to use these resources to seek control of political outcomes would ignore reality, not to mention market imperatives. Corporations already spend vast sums of corporate money to dominate political debate and outcomes.

The Impact of Corporate Money in Politics

The national Chamber of Commerce—the lobbying federation for the biggest corporations in America—ranks first in spending for lobbying in the past decade, spending literally hundreds of millions of dollars to determine what happens, and more often, what does not happen in Washington. Each year, the Chamber of Commerce spends hundreds of millions of dollars on lobbying and related political activity. And it was recently reported that the Chamber of Commerce promises to spend even more on the 2010 mid-term elections than it has previously.

In second place, the General Electric corporation spent $161 million on lobbying in the past decade. Pharmaceutical manufacturers gave more than $92 million to federal campaigns from 1989 to 2006. The financial services industry contributed $460 million to congressional and presidential candidates in 2008. And so on . . .

So what is the result of the corporate money onslaught in politics in recent decades, even before the *Citizens United* Court lifted all restraints? Americans feel deeply estranged from their government. According to the Pew Research Center, barely a third (34%) agree with the statement, "Most elected officials care what people like me think," a 10-point drop since 2002. No matter the issue or concern, whether one is a Democratic, Republican, Libertarian, Green or Independent, most people believe that our government

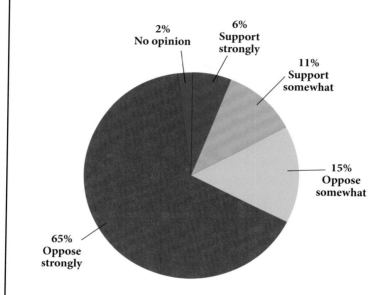

US Public Opinion on the *Citizens United* Ruling

"Do you support or oppose the recent ruling by the Supreme Court that says corporations and unions can spend as much money as they want to help political candidates win elections? Do you feel that way strongly or somewhat?"

2%
No opinion

6%
Support
strongly

11%
Support
somewhat

15%
Oppose
somewhat

65%
Oppose
strongly

TAKEN FROM: *Washington Post*-ABC News Poll, February 4–8, 2010. www.washingtonpost.com.

cannot seem to move on what a majority of the American people desire. More and more Americans have begun to associate corporate dominance in Washington with increasing powerlessness among people and dysfunction in our government.

The Impact on State and Local Elections

Citizens United not only bars Congress and the States from addressing this fundamental problem in our democracy; the decision promises to make the current state of our corporate-dominated politics look quaint by comparison. And the impacts go far beyond the federal Bipartisan Campaign Reform Act and federal elections. With no State even in the case before the Court, the *Citizens United* majority essentially erased the law of twenty-four states that banned corporate political expenditures. Thus, with virtually no consideration of the federalism implications and the circumstances in the States, State elections are now likely to be transformed.

In Montana, for example, before *Citizens United*, the average state legislator spent $17,000 to win election to the state legislature. On March 8, 2010, two corporations, citing *Citizens United*, sued the State of Montana to strike down a 1912 law providing that "A corporation may not make a contribution or expenditure in connection with a candidate or a political committee that supports or opposes a candidate or a political party." It is unlikely that state elections in Montana and elsewhere will remain accessible to most people, or that people will not be alienated by the transformation of state politics into contests among corporate-funded campaigns from competing corporate interests.[1]

Citizens United also will dramatically impair the impartiality, and the perceived impartiality, of justice in America. Twenty-one states have elected Supreme Court justices, and thirty-nine states elect at least some appellate or major trial court judges. Even before *Citizens United*, as former Justice Sandra Day O'Connor has said, "In too many states, judicial elections are becoming political prizefights where partisans and special interests seek to install judges who will answer to them instead of the law and the Constitution." Now corporations will have even greater ability to bring their financial resources to bear on those elections, further undermining the independence of the state judiciaries.

Finally, because *Citizens United* rests on the transformation of the expenditure of corporate general treasury funds into new "corporate speech" rights under the First Amendment, every elected official and person interested in representing their fellow citizens in America, from candidates for the presidency to candidates for the local school and water district, must now reckon with the power of corporate money to change the outcome of elections.

The New Corporate Rights Doctrine

Unfortunately, the damage to democracy from dubious "corporate speech" doctrines goes beyond *Citizens United* and beyond campaign finance. The disdain shown by the majority in *Citizens United* for the policy judgments of the people's elected representatives in Congress and the States is striking, but it reflects a growing disdain that has driven corporate speech activism in the judiciary for the past two decades.

Judicial respect for the people's choices about corporate regulation began to erode in the late 1970s and 1980s. The path to *Citizens United* follows from the fabrication beginning in those years of a corporate rights/commercial speech doctrine under the First Amendment. This new doctrine reached its zenith in *Citizens United*, but its damaging effects on democracy have already gone far beyond campaign finance laws.

For 200 years, there was no such thing as a right to corporate speech under the First Amendment. And the First Amendment did not prevent legislatures from enacting restrictions on corporate expenditures to influence elections. During the [Richard M.] Nixon Administration, however, in reaction to increasing legislative efforts to improve environmental, consumer, civil rights and public health laws, corporate executives began aggressively to push back for the creation of corporate rights. They followed a playbook spelled out in a memo from Lewis Powell, then a private attorney advising the Chamber of Commerce. President Nixon then appointed Lewis Powell to the Supreme Court. Over the following years, a divided Supreme Court, over powerful dissents by Justice William Rehnquist and others, transformed the First Amendment into a powerful tool for corporations seeking to evade democratic control and sidestep sound public welfare measures.

In 1978 several large corporations—including Gillette and Bank of Boston—challenged a Massachusetts prohibition on corporate expenditures to influence ballot questions. In an opinion authored by the former Chamber of Commerce lawyer, the now-Justice Powell, a 5–4 decision agreed with the corporate First Amendment claim, and cast aside the people's wish to keep corporate money out of Massachusetts citizens referenda. With increasing aggressiveness, the judiciary has since used this new corporate-rights doctrine to strike down state and federal laws regulating corporate conduct. Even a partial list of decisions striking down public laws shows the range of regulations falling to the new corporate rights doctrine, from those concerning clean and fair elections; to environmental protection and energy; to tobacco, alcohol, pharmaceuticals, and health care; to consumer protection, lotteries, and gambling; to race relations, and much more. . . .

The Notion of Corporate First Amendment Rights

More than ever before, corporate money in politics corrupts and distorts our political and legislative process, and shouts down the voice and speech and wishes of the American people. And even when a legislative victory in the people's interest occurs, armies of corporate lawyers go into battle to take the matter to a Supreme Court that has forgotten its place in the American experiment in self-government, and all too often, accedes to the corporate claims of immunity from regulation or control by the people.

It would be one thing if the Court's handcuffing of our ability to regulate corporate political money was an unfortunate but necessary price of liberty, or rooted in long-held Constitutional principles of free speech. We put up with views we find obnoxious and even repellent. We put up with rivers of crude and offensive expression in all media, and we tolerate every variety of dissent and opinion. That is a price we pay for freedom of speech.

But the notion of corporate First Amendment rights is not about freedom of speech, or even about any kind of speech or expression. It is about a kind of economic entity that we ourselves created and permit by legislation because we chose to do so for economic policy reasons. To appreciate how radical the corporate rights claim in *Citizens United* is, it helps to remember our history.

The Historical View of Corporate Power

The growing view among many people that we must restrain and control corporate power is not new in America and it is far from fringe. Throughout American history, at least until very recent times, that was the mainstream view. The American people have sought to keep corporate money out of elections virtually since the beginning of the Republic, and the root of the law struck down in *Citizens United* goes back to the 1907 Tilman Act, which banned corporate political contributions in federal campaigns.

For many years after the founding of our nation, state legislatures enacted corporate laws that allowed corporations, but only permitted these to be chartered for specific *public* purposes, and often limited the time period in which the corporate entity could operate. Restrictions on corporate purposes were the norm, and distrust and concern about the ability of corporations to grasp political power prevailed.

James Madison, often considered the primary author of our Constitution, viewed corporations as "a necessary evil" subject to "proper limitations and guards." Thomas Jefferson hoped to "crush in its birth the aristocracy of our moneyed corporations, which dare already to challenge our government to a trial of strength and bid defiance to the laws of our country." These views prevailed among Americans through the decades. Until recently, it was presidents and our leaders as much as those outside of politics who were vigilant about corporate power. . . .

The Need for a Constitutional Amendment

That day has come, and Congress and the States now are considering several worthwhile initiatives to address the Court's egregious error in *Citizens United*—public funding of elections, shareholder and governance reform, among others. As with so many previous challenges to democratic self-government, however, *Citizens United* also requires a 28th Constitutional Amendment to correct the Court, restore the First Amendment to the people's right, and remove unwarranted judicial controls on our lawmakers' oversight of corporate power.

Americans have amended the Constitution repeatedly to expand rather than dilute democratic participation of people in elections. Most of the seventeen amendments that followed the ten amendments of our Bill of Rights were adopted to expand democracy and eliminate barriers to democracy for everyone. One amendment even overruled the Supreme Court when the Court sided with economic power and held that Congress had no power to enact a graduated income tax. The people responded with an amendment making clear Congress did indeed have that power. We can and should do that again and end the misuse of the First Amendment by corporations to evade and invalidate reforms and public welfare measures.

Note

1. The US Supreme Court struck down the 1912 Montana law in June 2012.

| "We must, over the next few years,
define the boundaries of what is
acceptable in this brazen new world."

Freedom of Speech Can't Be Unlimited

Yasmin Alibhai-Brown

In the following viewpoint, Yasmin Alibhai-Brown argues that freedom of expression on the Internet should be limited. Alibhai-Brown claims that there have always been limits to freedom of expression and that the advent of the Internet has created the need to establish new boundaries for acceptable speech. Alibhai-Brown claims that hateful and untrue speech online can create real harms to real people and, therefore, must be restricted. Alibhai-Brown is a British journalist and a founding member of British Muslims for Secular Democracy.

As you read, consider the following questions:

1. Does the author share the view that the dropped obscenity case against Darryn Walker was a victory against censorship?
2. What is one example that Alibhai-Brown gives of laws that restrict freedom of speech?

3. What two mechanisms for self-regulation does the author endorse as necessary for restricting speech on the Internet?

Libertarians and free expression campaigners were jubilant last week. An obscenity case was due to be heard against Darryn Walker, a 35-year-old civil servant who had posted an essay on a website, titled "Girls (Scream) Aloud", imagining the sexual torture and mutilation of the each of the women who make up the pop group.

In his fantasy, they are slashed and dismembered and, according to Don Grubin, a consultant psychiatrist, the singers "are sexually aroused in spite of and, indeed, because of the humiliation, pain and domination". This apparently modern erotica known as "popslash". Cool, man.

The case was dropped and is celebrated as another important knock-back for censorship. Sadly I felt unable to join in with the good cheer. Something is deeply troubling about the validation given to Walker and those who think they have the right to say whatever they wish and excitedly share with others the thrills of extreme violence against women.

The formidable Geoffrey Robertson QC (who rose to fame fighting the case brought against *Oz*) is very pleased indeed. Jo Glanville, editor of Index Against Censorship (an organisation I support but not blindly) righteously asserts: "The prosecution should not have been brought in the first place. Since the landmark obscenity cases of the 1960s and 1970s, writers have been protected so they can explore the extremes of human behaviour. This case posed a serious threat to that freedom."

Hmmm. Is that so? So If Walker had written, say, the same fantasy but on the sexual torture of Anne Frank, would Index have backed him? Or if a wannabe Muslim fiction writer had done the same, would he have the right to "explore the extremes of human behaviour"? I hope the answer to both these hypothetical questions is No.

Freedom of speech is a precious right, fought for in Europe over many centuries, and still denied to billions of humans—as we have just witnessed in Iran and know to be true of China, African and Arab nations, Burma, and so on. Granted that in countries where the state oppresses and totally controls its populations, the people must find ways to subvert the controllers and criticise their oppressors.

Whistleblowers in institutions must also grab that freedom, so too family members thwarted by their own. But it is never an absolute entitlement, not unless you believe it is worth the resulting social discord and terrible individual wreckage.

We all exercise judgements on what we say or don't say in public. You stop yourself because you don't want to hurt people, or to instigate a street brawl. There are laws that sacrifice freedom of speech for a greater good—harmony between races, public safety, social gentility and so on. We accept libel and defamation laws (hated by hacks of course), national security injunctions and establishment secrets (loved by politicians) and underpinning all that is a general understanding of what would be inappropriate and hateful if expressed in public.

Not everybody agrees on where the lines should be, but most know there are lines. These restraints belong to a pre-internet era and cannot contain or temper the limitlessness of the web. And yet we must, over the next few years, define the boundaries of what is acceptable in this brazen new world.

It is all very well for Mr Walker to feel like a champion of human rights but what about the women in Girls Aloud, who are real, not imagined, and whose slow death can be enjoyed by pervs and killers? They have families, mums, perhaps, lovers, who too will be feeling caught in a web of horrors. The legal state is unsettled. Meanwhile the internet is exploding and explosive, having a real impact on real lives.

Last week I found myself being tailed through town by a weird bloke, who kept stopping me, once or twice seizing my elbow. Why, he demanded, did I want British soldiers killed and

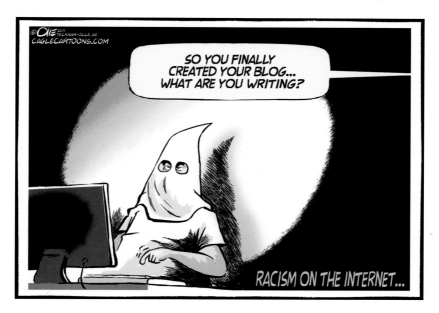

© 2011 OLLE JOHANSSON and Cagle Cartoons Inc.

hurt? This question has been coming at me via email for a few months. I couldn't understand why.

Someone told me my Wikipedia entry had quoted the NeoCon Doug Murray, who had attacked me in a book for writing: "There have been times when I have wanted more chaos, more shocks, more disorder to teach our side a lesson". To put this in context, what I actually wrote was: "The past months have been disquieting and challenging for many of us in the antiwar camp. I know and am ashamed to admit this, that there have been times when I have wanted more chaos, more shocks, more disorder to teach our side a lesson . . . The decent people of Iraq need optimism now not my distasteful ill-wishes for the only hope they have for the future." If this attack stayed in Murray's book it would have passed, but bloggers recently picked it up and it has been hell since.

Peter Tatchell tells me that lies are circulated about him and he receives constant threats. Polly Toynbee and others are subjected to mob fury for no good reason. Are we just supposed to put up with this behaviour because the web must be free?

Internet libel law is building up and internet service providers are put under pressure to remove sites where material is defamatory. Chatrooms and blogs are increasingly expected to be moderated. The defence of "innocent dissemination" may not survive.

In 2006, Ukip's Michael Keith won damages after joining a chatroom where anonymous postings smeared his character and in 2008 a CEO of a housing business got a large payout after a rival company carried out a malicious personal smear campaign against him. As the internet is transnational, awareness is growing that extraordinary care is needed to prevent legal action. Corporate liability, third party culpability are encouraging mechanisms for self-regulation. In my view some of this is necessary.

We don't yet have a really effective way of restraining material promoting racism, sexism, violence (except against children), homophobia, and other group hatreds. It must come if we are to make the best use of this amazing technology and not let it pull us down to a barbarism posing as freedom. That, I fear, is what has happened with Mr Walker and his spurious victory.

> *"I worry that identifying problems of abusive speech inevitably builds support for repressive legal 'solutions.'"*

Attempts to Limit Free Speech Online Can Lead to Repressive Solutions

Wendy Kaminer

In the following viewpoint, Wendy Kaminer argues that a recent campaign to stop misogynistic speech on the Internet is misguided. Kaminer points out that whereas government is not allowed to restrict speech, private online companies are. Nonetheless, Kaminer claims that companies who decide to restrict speech based on content run the risk of encouraging misguided legal restrictions and, moreover, she claims that such restrictions are ineffective in reducing misogyny. Kaminer is an author, lawyer, and civil libertarian.

As you read, consider the following questions:

1. According to Kaminer, should violent rhetoric be equated with violent action?
2. The author claims that the campaign to stamp out misogyny is not aimed at legal bans but at what?

3. What is Kaminer's opinion on efforts to distinguish hate speech from free speech?

Nothing much is unfamiliar about the latest feminist campaign to "stamp out" online misogyny. . . . The atavistic verbal abuse—including graphic rape fantasies—directed at some female bloggers is instantly recognizable; so is the insistence of some feminists that hate speech shouldn't be protected as free speech, that anonymous threats effectively "silence" women (who are then perversely characterized as the real victims of censorship), and that violent words are the equivalent of violent acts. As [psychotherapist and social critic] Susie Orbach declares, "The threat of sexual violence is violence itself . . . and it's meant to shut people up."

The Campaign to Restrict Online Speech

This is hyperbole, like much of the abuse of which women complain. You don't need a lot of empathy to understand that being targeted by deranged descriptions of violent assaults can be deeply unsettling. But you only need a little common sense to know that violent rhetoric does not equal violent action, and that every woman who equates words with actions would still rather be the subject of a metaphoric assault than an actual one. Nor should you need a law degree to recognize the difficulty of defining "abusive" speech and the dangers of censoring it. Intentional targeted threats of violence, or "true threats," may be prohibited. But even in these extreme cases, courts struggle to distinguish between actionable threats and protected advocacy or overheated rhetoric, while some women protesting their online abuse don't even acknowledge the distinctions.

The stamp out misogyny campaign isn't necessarily aimed at securing legal bans on misogynist speech (although it includes pleas for legal interventions and could easily inspire some). It seems focused more on encouraging private actions by private owners and gatekeepers: Facebook is exhorted to "ban sexist pages;" online forums are urged to ban anonymous postings and filter abusive comments (as major sites do.) This is not, then, a simple debate about censorship, pitting essential and established First Amendment rights against some imaginary civil right not to be offended or viciously heckled. It's a debate about the private prerogatives and preferences of owners, producers, and consumers of new media.

The only formal rights involved in this particular debate are the rights of private entities to control access to their sites and set the terms of whatever debates are aired there. Anonymity may be a treasured online tradition (however recent), but it is not a right, except in the public sphere: the state can't legally stop you from publishing or posting anonymously, but the owner of a privately owned site or publication can decline to give you access.

The Danger of Private Restrictions

In fact, you don't have a right to post comments under your own name, much less anonymously, just as you don't have a right to force a newspaper to publish your letter to the editor. Yes, an online site has the capacity to post comments that a print publication lacks; but to suggest that the capacity to post your comment, anonymously or not, imbues you with a right to have it posted is a bit like suggesting that your capacity to copy and paste this column imbues you with a right to appropriate it, or that the ease with which you can enter an unlocked house gives you the right to commit a burglary. Your right to engage in an activity is not determined by your ability to do so. This is not an argument to end anonymity or increase monitoring of comments. It is simply an effort to distinguish between rights, prerogatives, and permissions in the battle over online speech.

Libertarians considering the prospect of additional, private restrictions on speech may be torn between their affection for raucous, open, free debate, and their sympathy for the rights of private parties to control the debates that occur on their properties. Personally, I'm ambivalent toward the stamp out misogyny campaign. I don't believe that misogyny will be eliminated or significantly diminished by private suppression of misogynist online speech. I worry that identifying problems of abusive speech inevitably builds support for repressive legal "solutions." And I shudder at nonsensical efforts to distinguish "hate speech" from free speech; freedom for the speech you like would merely be redundant. But when women complain about speech they consider abusive or downright frightening, I have to say, welcome to the fray. You may mock them for complaining, but "complaint" is just another word for protest. Besides, women who speak out against misogyny can't claim to have been silenced by it.

Periodical and Internet Sources Bibliography

The following articles have been selected to supplement the diverse views presented in this chapter.

Trevor Burrus	"'Wrong' Speech Is Also Free Speech: *Citizens United* at Two," *Huffington Post*, January 24, 2012. www.huffingtonpost.com.
Denzel Condrington	"Racism Flourishes Online," *Los Angeles Sentinel*, August 19, 2010.
Charles C.W. Cooke	"The Crime of Leafleting," *National Review*, January 13, 2012.
Jonah Goldberg	"Between Garbage and Gold," *National Review*, March 4, 2011.
Jill Lawless	"Twitter Tirades Test Limits of Freedom of Speech," *Huffington Post*, November 23, 2010. www.huffingtonpost.com.
Michelle Malkin	"The Hate Speech Inquisition," *National Review*, January 19, 2011.
William Murchinson	"The Limits of Free Speech: Whatever Happened to Common Sense?," *Imaginative Conservative*, March 7, 2011. www.imaginativeconservative.org.
Erna Paris	"There Are Limits to Free Expression," *Globe and Mail* (Toronto), October 28, 2011.
Bernie Sanders and Robert Weissman	"We the People," *Huffington Post*, January 20, 2012. www.huffingtonpost.com.
Robert Skidelsky	"Free Speech Under Siege," Project Syndicate, June 21, 2011. www.project-syndicate.org.
Matt Welch	"The 'Costs' of Free Speech: Consequentialism and the First Amendment Don't Mix," *Reason*, July 2010.

CHAPTER 2

Does the First Amendment Require Separation of Church and State?

Chapter Preface

Freedom of religion is one of the foundational civil liberties of the United States. The First Amendment to the US Constitution guarantees that "Congress shall make no law respecting an establishment of religion, or prohibiting the exercise thereof." The first clause is known as the Establishment Clause and prohibits the government from establishing or endorsing any religion. The second clause is known as the Free Exercise Clause and prohibits the government from barring the exercise of religion by citizens. Together these clauses guarantee religious freedom in the United States, simultaneously forbidding government from promoting or favoring any particular religion while allowing people to practice religion if they so choose. Balancing these two principles in the public sphere has been fraught with controversy since the nation's founding: Neutrality toward religion must avoid hostility toward religion and accommodation of religion must not become government endorsement of religion. Over the years the US Supreme Court has made several key decisions clarifying how these two clauses of the First Amendment protect religious freedom.

The Establishment Clause guarantees that the government will not establish an official religion. A common way of expressing the concept that government should stay out of the business of religion is that of "building a wall of separation between church and State," an idea expressed by Thomas Jefferson in 1802 in a letter to the Danbury Baptist Association. The court's foremost case defining this separation of church and state under the Establishment Clause is *Lemon v. Kurtzman* (1971), which articulated what has come to be known as the *Lemon* test. The court held that three elements are necessary for a law to be constitutional under the Establishment Clause: "First, the statute must have a secular legislative purpose; second, its principal or primary effect must be one that neither advances nor inhibits religion; . . . [and] finally, the statute must not foster an excessive government entanglement with religion." The *Lemon* test continues to be used in the courts, although not without debate concerning what the test allows and disallows.

The Free Exercise Clause prevents government from prohibiting the exercise of religion. The exercise of religion may involve belief, speech, and conduct but, as the court recognized in 1940 in its ruling in *Cantwell v. Connecticut*: "The Amendment embraces two concepts—freedom to believe and freedom to act. The first is absolute, but, in the nature of things, the second cannot be." In other words, whereas freedom of religious belief is absolute, the freedom to engage in religious speech and conduct is not. An early court decision regarding the Free Exercise Clause illustrates this distinction between belief and conduct. In 1878 the court ruled in *Reynolds v. United States* that the Free Exercise Clause does not protect the right to polygamy—having more than one spouse—even if one's religion demands the practice: Laws are made for the government of actions, and while they cannot interfere with mere religious belief and opinions, they may with practices. Suppose one believed that human sacrifices were a necessary part of religious worship; would it be seriously contended that the civil government under which he lived could not interfere to prevent a sacrifice? Thus, the Constitution allows for the exercise of religion to be limited by government in situations where religious conduct is seen as harming others or otherwise at odds with legitimate government interests.

Just how one ought to understand the constitutional guarantee of religious freedom continues to be a source of controversy in the United States. Even the idea of the separation of church and state is full of controversy: some argue that government neutrality toward religion has gone too far. Elizabeth Dole inspired many supporters and critics when, at the 2004 Republican convention, she said, "The Constitution guarantees freedom of religion, not freedom from religion," expressing an idea endorsed by many conservatives. Equally passionate on the other side of the debate, however, are those who argue that a stark separation of church and state should be maintained. Resolving this issue in the public sphere, especially as it pertains to public schools, is an ongoing source of debate.

| "*The attack on separation of church and state involves twisting words and reading history backwards, and it involves making an inconvenient part of the Constitution disappear.*"

The First Amendment Requires Separation of Church and State

Garrett Epps

In the following viewpoint, Garrett Epps argues that despite the recent attack on the concept of separation of church and state, the idea of separation has strong historical and constitutional support. Epps claims that historical examination of the views of the Founding Fathers shows that the First Amendment was always meant to require separation of church and state. Furthermore, Epps contends that a lack of separation is dangerous not only because it threatens civil peace, but also because it threatens freedom of religion. Epps is a professor of law at the University of Baltimore, as well as a novelist and a journalist.

As you read, consider the following questions:

1. According to Epps, opponents of the separation of church and state believe that the restriction on "establishment of religion" in the First Amendment means what?

2. In addition to the text of the First Amendment, what article of the US Constitution does the author cite in support of the idea of separation of church and state?
3. Epps credits what theologian as the original source of the metaphor of separation of church and state?

Christine O'Donnell died for the far right's constitutional sins. In the fall of 2010, the dilettante-witch-turned-Tea-Party-Senate-candidate sneered at her opponent, Democrat Chris Coons, when he pointed out in a debate that the First Amendment to the Constitution prohibits "an establishment of religion."

> O'Donnell: Let me just clarify: You're telling me that the separation of church and state is found in the First Amendment?
>
> Coons: Government shall make no [law respecting an] establishment of religion.
>
> O'Donnell: That's in the First Amendment?

The Attack on the Separation of Church and State

O'Donnell paid with a thumping repudiation at the polls even in a year of far-right victories. But her mistake was not a random one. As [radio talk-show host] Rush Limbaugh explained in defense of O'Donnell, "She was incredulous that somebody was saying that the Constitution said there must be separation between church and state. Those words are not in the Constitution." In 2006, [Republican congresswoman] Michele Bachmann warned a Christian group that public schools "are teaching children that there is separation of church and state, and I am here to tell you that is a myth." This year's [2011] right-wing pinup, amateur historian David Barton, devotes his book *Original Intent: The Courts, the Constitution, and Religion* to the proposition that separation of church and state is "a relatively recent concept rather than . . . a long-standing constitutional principle."

The attack on separation of church and state involves twisting words and reading history backwards, and it involves making an inconvenient part of the Constitution disappear. Most ardently espoused by loud foes of "big government," the attack aims to place government in charge of Americans' spiritual lives.

The idea is that the Framers desired a Christian nation, in which government oversaw the spiritual development of the people by reminding them of their religious duties and subsidizing the churches where they worship. "Establishment of religion," in this reading, simply means that no single Christian *denomination* could be officially favored. But official prayers, exhortations to faith, religious monuments, and participation by church bodies in government were all part of the "original intent," the argument goes.

Because the *words* "separation of church and state" do not appear in the Constitution, the argument runs, the document provides for *merger* of the two.

The History of Separation

It's bosh: ahistorical, untextual, illogical.

Patriots like Thomas Jefferson, John Adams, and James Madison were profoundly skeptical about the claims of what they called "revealed religion." As children of the 18th-century Enlightenment, they stressed reason and scientific observation as a means of discovering the nature of "Providence," the power that had created the world. Jefferson, for example, took a pair of scissors to the Christian New Testament and cut out every passage that suggested a divine origin and mission for Jesus. In their long correspondence, Jefferson and John Adams swapped frequent witticisms about the presumption of the clergy. ("Every Species of these Christians would persecute Deists," Adams wrote on June 25, 1813, "as soon as either Sect would persecute another, if it had unchecked and unbalanced power. Nay, the

Deists would persecute Christians, and Atheists would persecute Deists, with as unrelenting Cruelty, as any Christians would persecute them or one another. Know thyself, Human Nature!") As president, Adams signed (and the U.S. Senate approved) the 1797 Treaty with Tripoli, which reassured that Muslim nation that "the Government of the United States of America is not, in any sense, founded on the Christian religion."

James Madison, the father of both the Constitution and the First Amendment, consistently warned against any attempt to blend endorsement of Christianity into the law of the new nation. "Who does not see that the same authority which can establish Christianity, in exclusion of all other Religions," he wrote in his *Memorial and Remonstrance Against Religious Assessments* in 1785, "may establish with the same ease any particular sect of Christians, in exclusion of all other Sects?" Unlike the Articles of Confederation, the Constitution conspicuously omits any reference to God.

The Idea of Separation

The words "separation of church and state" are not in the text; the idea of separation is. Article VI provides that all state and federal officials "shall be bound by oath or affirmation, to support this Constitution; but *no religious test shall ever be required* as a qualification to any office or public trust under the United States." The First Amendment's Establishment Clause (which Christine O'Donnell had apparently not read) provides that "Congress shall make no law respecting an establishment of religion"—meaning that not only no church but no "religion" could be made the official faith of the United States. Finally the Free Exercise Clause provides that Congress shall not make laws "prohibiting the free exercise" of religion. (These prohibitions were extended to state governments by the Fourteenth Amendment, whose framers in 1866 wanted to make sure that the states maintained free, democratic systems instead of the old antebellum slave oligarchies that spawned the Civil War.)

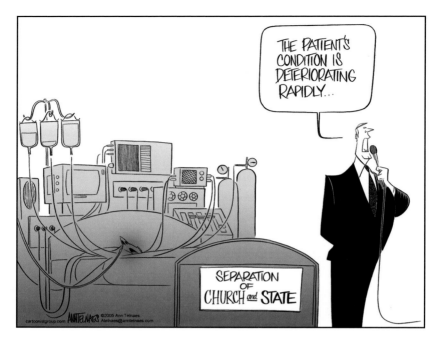

If government can't require its officials to support a church, may not support a church itself, and may not interfere with the worship or belief of any church, is there a serious argument that church and state are *not* separate?

The attack on separation began as an attack on a letter by Thomas Jefferson to the Danbury Baptist Association, dated Jan. 1, 1802. Jefferson assured the Baptists that "I contemplate with sovereign reverence that act of the whole American people which declared that their legislature should 'make no law respecting an establishment of religion, or prohibiting the free exercise thereof,' thus building a wall of separation between Church & State." In 1985, then-Justice William Rehnquist wrote that "unfortunately the Establishment Clause has been expressly freighted with Jefferson's misleading metaphor for nearly 40 years."

100

Protection of Religion and Society

But this argument ignores a historical fact. It's not Jefferson's metaphor. Even in 1802, separation was already deeply rooted in American religious history. In 1644, the American theologian Roger Williams, founder of the first Baptist congregation in the British New World, coined the phrase to signify the protection that the church needed in order to prevent misuse and corruption by political leaders: "The church of the Jews under the Old Testament in the type and the church of the Christians under the New Testament in the antitype were both separate from the world; and when they have opened a gap in the hedge or wall of separation between the garden of the church and the wilderness of the world, God hath ever broke down the wall itself, removed the candlestick, and made his garden a wilderness."

It is this concept—that use by political leaders of religion for their own ends was a danger both to the faithful and to the peace of society—that the Constitution embodies. James Madison wrote that government involvement with the church "implies either that the civil magistrate is a competent judge of religious truth; or that he may employ religion as an engine of civil policy. The first is an arrogant pretension falsified by the contradictory opinions of rulers in all ages, and throughout the world: the second an unhallowed perversion of the means of salvation."

The current right-wing drive to harness the power of government to bring souls to Christ is dangerous and un-American. As no less conservative a figure than Sandra Day O'Connor wrote in 2005: "Those who would renegotiate the boundaries between church and state must therefore answer a difficult question: why would we trade a system that has served us so well for one that has served others so poorly?"

"The First Amendment gives religious Americans preferential treatment: in the exercise of their religion, they are specifically protected from government interference."

The First Amendment Protects Religious Expression Unless It Is Coercive

Antony Barone Kolenc

In the following viewpoint, Antony Barone Kolenc argues that recent attempts to exclude all religion from public life will not be successful. Kolenc contends that the majority on the US Supreme Court correctly endorses the view that religion was never meant to be excluded from public life. He predicts the court will adopt a view of the separation of church and state where only coercive government endorsement of religion is unconstitutional. Kolenc is an attorney with the US Air Force Judge Advocate General Corps and an adjunct faculty member at Saint Leo University. This viewpoint originally appeared in America, *a national Catholic magazine.*

Antony Barone Kolenc, "The Court at a Crossroads: A New Majority Enters the Culture Wars," *America Magazine*, vol. 198, no. 14, April 28, 2008. Copyright © 2008 by America Magazine. All rights reserved. Reproduced by permission.

As you read, consider the following questions:

1. Which five US Supreme Court justices does the author identify as forming a Catholic majority?
2. What test does the author suggest will replace the "*Lemon* test" for determining church-state questions?
3. Kolenc claims that the US Supreme Court has shown tolerance for nonsectarian prayer in what setting?

An atheist in California has again sued to remove the words "under God" from the Pledge of Allegiance and "In God We Trust" from all U.S. currency. A student in Vermont is suing her school for refusing to recognize her Christian club. An Illinois high school freshman has challenged her school's "moment of silence." And, of course, Christmas 2007 brought another spike in religion-related complaints—protests about public school choirs singing religious songs and demands that Nativity scenes be removed from outside town halls. Religion-based lawsuits like these have continued to multiply in recent years.

A Catholic Majority on the Court

As this most recent batch of cases works its way through the legal system, however, those involved may find themselves before a Supreme Court that is ready to redefine some of the controversial boundaries between church and state. Big change may be coming in America's culture war—a legal shift that could alter the so-called separation between church and state. And a Roman Catholic majority on the United States Supreme Court may be the driving force behind it.

In the past 50 years, the nine justices on the U.S. Supreme Court have struggled to solve divisive religious issues brought under the Constitution's First Amendment guarantee of freedom of religion. The result? A confusing patchwork of legal mumbo jumbo. These cases—often decided by a vote of 5 to 4—have limited how government is permitted to recognize God. Justice

Sandra Day O'Connor (a social moderate and the first woman to serve on the court) often wielded that decisive fifth, swing vote on matters of religion.

O'Connor is retired now, replaced by Samuel Alito, the fifth Catholic justice on the present Supreme Court. Justice Alito has joined Anthony Kennedy, Antonin Scalia, Clarence Thomas and Chief Justice John Roberts to form the first Catholic majority in the court's history.

Will this change the course of court decisions? These five justices are likely to vote together, but not primarily because they share the Catholic faith. Instead, they share a conservative judicial philosophy that values the role of religion in our nation's traditions and in its moral foundation.

The Establishment Clause

"Congress shall make no law respecting an establishment of religion." These first 10 words of the First Amendment—known as the establishment clause—were placed in the Constitution by our founding fathers. What do they mean?

It is generally agreed that these words mean the federal government cannot set up an official religion, as England had done with the Anglican Church. Nor can the state coerce its citizens through taxation or other laws to support any particular religion. But the conservative justices argue further that our nation was built on faith in a supreme being—a God whom the founders never intended to exclude from public life.

The Declaration of Independence says our Creator endowed us with certain inalienable rights, among these are "life, liberty and the pursuit of happiness." And John Adams, a founder and the second president, noted, "Our Constitution was made only for a moral and religious people. It is wholly inadequate to the government of any other." To this end, the First Amendment gives religious Americans preferential treatment: in the exercise of their religion, they are specifically protected from government interference.

On the other hand, the four more liberal justices on the court view the Constitution as a living document that has evolved from 18th-century thought. In their view, modernity requires a stricter separation between church and state, with very little (or no) government involvement with religion. They fear that some Americans—atheists and those practicing alternative religions—could be treated as second-class citizens.

A Different Approach to Church and State

On today's Supreme Court, Justice Antonin Scalia and Justice Anthony Kennedy stand out, each for a different reason. Justice Scalia is undoubtedly the most outspoken voice on establishment clause issues. He has been a longtime critic of the court's rulings, arguing for greater tolerance of religion in the public arena. A persuasive advocate, Scalia is often joined in his campaign by Roberts, Thomas and Alito.

Justice Kennedy, on the other hand, has a special role to play: he is the new swing vote on establishment clause issues. This means he will usually be the decisive fifth vote that carries the day, one way or the other. Although Kennedy is generally conservative on matters of religion, he is less so than his fellow Catholics on the court. Kennedy voted to uphold *Roe v. Wade* [1973], which established abortion as a fundamental right. He also authored the 2003 opinion that for the first time recognized legal protections for homosexual persons. Justice Scalia, on the other hand, voted opposite to Kennedy on both issues.

Changes in the area of church-state law will occur only to the extent that Justice Kennedy and his swing vote allow. But we can expect Kennedy to join the other four conservative justices in creating a more practical, common sense approach to matters of church and state. Most significantly, the court is likely to abandon the controversial "Lemon test," a point of reference for deciding church-state questions. This complicated three-part test has been widely criticized as both ill-conceived and inconsistently applied.

In its place, expect to see a new judicial measuring rod—the "coercion test." Using this tool, the court will decide whether the state has coerced its citizens to support or participate in any religion or religious exercise. Though key constitutional protections will continue even while the externals change, applying this simpler test may result in striking changes from the current way the court views some issues.

The Ten Commandments on Public Grounds

Most significant, the new majority may alter the rules governing public displays, especially depictions of the Ten Commandments and Nativity scenes at Christmas.

In recent years, monuments with the Ten Commandments inscribed on them have been a flashpoint for litigation when set up on government property. Activist groups have successfully challenged displays of the commandments on courthouse walls and town squares. In 2005, the Supreme Court put out a muddled batch of opinions on this matter, with Justice O'Connor voting to remove the commandments from a courthouse in Kentucky.

Now that Justice O'Connor has departed, however, expect to see future decisions going the other way. Justice Kennedy will likely join the other four conservative justices in permitting displays of the Ten Commandments on public grounds. Such displays would be accepted as an acknowledgment of religion's contribution to American heritage. The court could find that such exhibits do not coerce observers to participate in any particular religion.

Would there be any limits on displaying the commandments? Certainly. The court would still prevent them from being used by the government to evangelize. For instance, a state will not be able to use the commandments to advocate conversion to Christianity.

Christmas Displays on Public Grounds

Another departure from precedent involves Christmas displays on public grounds. This overly complicated area of the law is due for

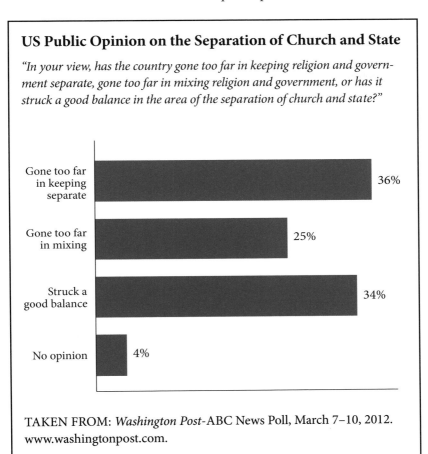

US Public Opinion on the Separation of Church and State

"In your view, has the country gone too far in keeping religion and government separate, gone too far in mixing religion and government, or has it struck a good balance in the area of the separation of church and state?"

Gone too far in keeping separate — 36%

Gone too far in mixing — 25%

Struck a good balance — 34%

No opinion — 4%

TAKEN FROM: *Washington Post*-ABC News Poll, March 7–10, 2012. www.washingtonpost.com.

an overhaul. Under the current rules, government offices are severely limited in how they set up decorations, such as the Christian Nativity or the Jewish menorah. Displays now need to be watered down, for instance, so that no one will think the government is sending a religious message. This typically means that the baby Jesus is surrounded by Santa Claus, "holiday" trees and the like, to avoid appearing in any way to endorse Christianity. As Justice Kennedy has written, rules like this unfairly punish majority religions by giving them "the status of least favored faiths so as to avoid any possible risk of offending members of minority religions."

But under the "coercion test," this hypersensitive policy may go the way of the dinosaur. In future cases, the court will decide whether such displays coerce people to participate in religious exercise. The justices could rule that erecting a crèche [Nativity scene] at Christmas is not coercive—it simply recognizes the importance of the Nativity to a traditional national holiday.

So those endless December complaints about religious symbols may now be short-circuited by the Supreme Court. Christ may be permitted back in Christmas—even in the public square or high school choir.

Religious Clubs in Public Schools

Sometimes public schools are unnecessarily concerned about allowing religious student clubs. Principals are afraid of improperly endorsing religion. But this fear is not well founded.

In a series of equal rights cases, the court has ruled that both religious and secular groups should have the same access to public facilities. To forbid equal access would be to discriminate simply because of a group's religious identity. For the same reason, religious organizations are permitted to accept generally available public financial aid.

Under the new majority, these rules will be continued and possibly enhanced. For example, the court has already turned back one challenge to President George W. Bush's faith-based initiatives program, which permits aid to religious groups performing secular work, like helping the homeless. This and similar programs will survive under the coercion test.

What does all this mean? In practical terms, the Vermont student whose Christian club was rejected by her high school has a strong chance of prevailing in her case.

Prayer in Public Schools

Another controversial issue involves official prayer, especially in a public school setting. The courts have previously rejected prayer and moments of silence in schools, believing them to be endorsements of religion among the "impressionable young."

Outside the school setting, however, the Supreme Court has shown tolerance for nonsectarian prayer by government officials. The court has allowed legislators, for instance, to start their sessions with official prayer, as they have done for centuries. Justice Scalia in particular has noted the longstanding American tradition "to acknowledge and beseech the blessing of God as a people, and not just as individuals." The new majority will likely continue to permit such prayers by officials, as long as no coercion occurs.

But what of the Illinois student's challenge to her school's moment of silence? It is unclear whether the court will now allow such in-school periods of reflection. In past cases, Justice Kennedy has voted to strike down laws that bring prayer into public schools. He views school activities as obligatory and subtly coercive because of peer pressure on students to conform. Justice Scalia disagrees, arguing that "speech is not coercive; the listener may do as he likes." In the end, the fate of moments of silence may depend on whether Justice Kennedy views the policy as sanctioning official prayer in school. [The US Court of Appeals for the Seventh Circuit upheld the school's moment-of-silence practice as constitutional and the US Supreme Court refused to review the case—ed.]

One thing is virtually certain: the California atheist's attempts to strike the words "under God" and "In God We Trust" from American public life will fail. Neither Kennedy nor the other conservative justices seem to think these words are coercive or a form of prayer. Indeed, the court will likely affirm the government's recognition of our country's long-held traditions and the role of religion in developing America into a great nation. [The appeals court denied the atheist's claims and the Supreme Court refused to review the case—ed.]

*"Educators' overriding concern should
be to protect students from religious
indoctrination by school personnel or
classmates and to ensure that school
policies don't unduly interfere with
students' practice or expression of
their beliefs."*

Schools Must Protect Students from Religious Indoctrination While Allowing Religious Expression

Martha McCarthy

*In the following viewpoint, Martha McCarthy claims that US
Supreme Court decisions involving church-state cases in public
schools illustrate that educators must avoid the establishment of
religion forbidden by the Establishment Clause of the First Amendment, while also upholding students' rights to free expression of religion guaranteed by the Free Exercise Clause. McCarthy explains
key court decisions on the issue and notes that some areas of law
are not settled. McCarthy chairs the Department of Educational
Leadership and Policy Studies at Indiana University.*

Martha McCarthy, "Beyond the Wall of Separation: Church-State Concerns in Public
Schools," *Phi Delta Kappan*, vol. 90, no. 10, June 2009, p. 714. Copyright © 2009 by Phi
Delta Kappa. Reprinted with permission of Phi Delta Kappa International, www.pdkintl.
org. All rights reserved.

As you read, consider the following questions:

1. McCarthy claims that from 1971 to 1992, the US Supreme Court consistently applied what standard in reviewing cases on religion in public schools?
2. According to the author, why was an Alabama law regarding silent meditation in Alabama public schools struck down in 1985?
3. In what way must educators be careful not to violate the Free Speech Clause in dealing with religious issues in public schools, according to the author?

Few controversies involving public schools have been more volatile than those pertaining to religious issues. Since the mid-20th century, schools have been the setting for some major church-state decisions rendered by the U.S. Supreme Court.

The First Amendment to the U.S. Constitution states in part that "Congress shall make no law respecting an establishment of religion" (Establishment Clause) "or prohibiting the free exercise thereof" (Free Exercise Clause). Our nation was unique in including a constitutional provision prohibiting religious establishment. The Supreme Court's first significant Establishment Clause decision in 1947 involved state aid to religious schools and introduced Thomas Jefferson's metaphor of a wall of separation between church and state. This metaphor became prominent in church-state litigation for more than 30 years, though references to the wall have been noticeably missing in recent Supreme Court decisions.

Supreme Court Cases on Religion in Schools

Most education cases have involved claims under the Establishment Clause, but some lawsuits have asserted that neutral government policies abridge the Free Exercise Clause by placing a burden on the exercise of religious beliefs without an overriding justification. In the leading free exercise case involving schools, *Wisconsin v. Yoder* [1972], the Supreme Court ruled that there was no compelling interest for the state to place a burden on the dictates of the Amish faith by requiring Amish youth to attend school beyond 8th grade.

In the early 1960s, the Supreme Court rendered two seminal decisions in which it prohibited public schools from sponsoring daily prayer and Bible reading, concluding that such activities advanced religion in violation of the Establishment Clause. Students' voluntary participation in the religious activities was irrelevant; school sponsorship of the devotional activities was sufficient to abridge the First Amendment. These decisions have generated a half century of subsequent litigation, legislative reactions, and efforts to amend the U.S. Constitution to authorize school prayer.

From 1971 until 1992, the Supreme Court consistently applied a stringent standard, referred to as the Lemon test, under which the challenged government action could satisfy the First Amendment only if it had a secular purpose, neither advanced nor impeded religion, and avoided excessive government entanglement with religion. Recently, the Court has seemed more inclined to assess whether an objective observer would view the challenged action as endorsing religion, and on occasion the Court has required evidence of religious coercion to find an Establishment Clause violation.

Applying the Establishment Clause, the Supreme Court has continued to strike down school-sponsored religious activities, such as posting the Ten Commandments in classrooms, having clergy deliver graduation prayers, and holding student elections to authorize student-led prayers at sporting events. But the Court also has emphasized that private religious expression does not abridge the Establishment Clause and that the Free Speech Clause requires the equal treatment of private religious and secular expression. Not only has the Supreme Court recognized this principle under the First Amendment, but also the Equal

Access Act (EAA), adopted by Congress in 1984, has augmented the constitutional standard. The EAA specifies that if secondary schools receiving federal aid create a forum for student expression during noninstructional time, student groups cannot be denied access based on the religious, political, or philosophical content of their expression. The concepts of equal access for religious groups and equal treatment of religious expression seem to have replaced the metaphor of a wall of separation between church and state.

Church-state disputes involving schools often divide communities, and there are no signs of these controversies dissipating in the near future.

The Issue of Student-Led Devotionals

In response to the Supreme Court decision striking down clergy-led prayers in public school graduation ceremonies in *Lee v. Weisman* [1992], creative strategies have been proposed to include devotional activities in graduation exercises and other public school events. Most of these strategies have involved student-led prayers, and courts have been called on to identify when religious expression in public schools is private and thus does not implicate the Establishment Clause.

Some school districts have designated the graduation ceremony as a forum for student expression. Student-delivered religious messages have been upheld in such forums if the students have been chosen by academic standing or other neutral criteria and if school authorities have not reviewed their speeches. However, where school districts maintain control of all aspects of the graduation ceremony, courts have endorsed censorship of proselytizing speeches to avoid an Establishment Clause violation. The central consideration is whether the school has explicitly created a forum for student expression or has retained control over the graduation ceremony.

It is doubtful that school districts can allow students to vote on whether to have student-led devotionals at school-sponsored events because delegating decisions to students does not reduce the Establishment Clause violation. In 2000, the Supreme Court invalidated a Texas school district's policy that authorized elections to determine whether student-led devotionals would be delivered before public school football games. The Court concluded that such expression at a school event on school property and representing the student body under the supervision of school personnel could not be considered private speech. Noting that the purpose of the Bill of Rights is to remove certain subjects from the political process, the Court held that student elections to determine if prayers will be said ensures that minority views never will be heard. Yet, the Court majority emphasized that only state sponsorship of devotionals violates the Establishment Clause. Subsequently, the Eleventh Circuit broadly interpreted free speech protection of student-initiated religious expression, recognizing that all student speech in public schools cannot be equated with expression representing the public school.

One indication of movement toward government accommodation of religion is the Supreme Court's conclusion that the Free Speech Clause requires public schools to allow devotional meetings during non-instructional time if any community groups are given access to the school. Public schools do not have to create a forum for community meetings; but once they do, they cannot discriminate against religious expression even if the devotional meetings are immediately after school and target elementary students.

Restrictions on Proselytizing Activities

Establishment Clause restrictions on government promotion of religious creeds are particularly important in public schools, given the vulnerable and captive student audience. Educators cannot lead prayer sessions, display or distribute religious materials, use religious references in instruction, wear proselytizing clothes, or disregard curriculum components for religious reasons. The judiciary has recognized that public educators don't have a right to use the influence of their positions to impose sectarian beliefs on students.

Laws or policies calling for a moment of silence for prayer or meditation in public schools, which currently are on the books in most states, have been challenged as proselytizing students. Although in 1985 the Supreme Court struck down an Alabama law that added the word "prayer" to a silent meditation statute, ruling that it was designed to advance religion, most courts have rejected recent challenges to such laws, noting that a period for quiet reflection is a good management technique to settle students. However, these laws remain controversial, and courts carefully assess their legislative history to determine whether they are designed to advance religion. In 2009, the Fifth Circuit upheld a Texas law mandating that public schools observe a moment of silence, but a federal district court struck down an Illinois statute that compelled each teacher to observe a period of silence for prayer or reflection. [The appeals court, however, later reversed, finding the period of silence constitutional.]

Some recent legal activity has focused on allegations that public schools are proselytizing students by reciting the Pledge of Allegiance each day. In 1943, the Supreme Court ruled that students have a right to opt out of the pledge, but this issue still is generating litigation. More controversial is whether the pledge can be said at all in public schools because of the phrase "under God." Several courts have found that the contested phrase represents permissible ceremonial or civic deism and has lost its religious meaning. But the Ninth Circuit attracted national attention and considerable negative reaction when it held that reciting the pledge with this phrase in public schools violated the Establishment Clause. The court reasoned that "under God" was added to the pledge in 1954 for religious reasons—to promote Christianity and combat atheistic communism. The Supreme Court avoided the merits of the case by reversing the Ninth Circuit because the noncustodial parent lacked standing to sue on behalf of his daughter. A similar challenge is under review, so

Court Review Under the Establishment and Free Exercise Clauses of the US Constitution

To determine whether a state action, or more specifically in this context, to determine whether the action of a public school official runs afoul of the Establishment Clause, reviewing courts apply a three-part test developed by the Supreme Court in *Lemon v. Kurtzman* [1971]. These three prongs are commonly called the purpose, effect, and entanglement prongs of the *Lemon* test and can be summarized as follows. First, to be constitutional, the public school action must have a primary secular purpose. Second, the primary or principal effect of the public school action must be one that neither advances nor inhibits religion. Third, the public school action must not result in an excessive entanglement of government with religion.

To determine whether the conduct of a public school official runs afoul of the Free Exercise Clause, reviewing courts employ several tests. The Supreme Court has interpreted the Free Exercise Clause as meaning "first and foremost, the right to believe and profess whatever religious doctrine one desires." This means that a state actor, such as a public school, "may not, for example, (1) compel affirmation of religious beliefs; (2) punish the expression of religious doctrines it believes to be false; (3) impose special disabilities on the basis of religious views or religious status; or (4) lend its power to one side or the other in controversies over religious authorities or dogma."

Anne Marie Lofaso, Americans United
for Separation of Church and State,
2009.

the Supreme Court may have another opportunity to address the merits of this issue.

Although allowing public school teachers to proselytize students violates the Establishment Clause, the Supreme Court has ruled that students can be released to receive religious instruction off school grounds. Also, the Court has emphasized that it is permissible and even desirable in public schools to teach the Bible and other religious documents from a literary, cultural, or historical perspective. But Bible study courses cannot be controlled by outside groups or be a ploy to advance sectarian beliefs.

Religion and the Curriculum

Students have been successful in asserting religious reasons in order to be excused from some assignments and activities (e.g., folk dancing, reading a specific novel) as long as an alternative assignment can satisfy the school's objectives and the exemption doesn't interfere with the student's education or the school program. Most of these requests are handled informally, so they don't often generate legal challenges. However, some parents have gone beyond seeking exemptions for their children, contending that aspects of the curriculum should be eliminated for religious reasons. Sex education, values education, and other components of the curriculum, as well as instructional materials, have been challenged as promoting nontheistic religious creeds or degrading Christianity in violation of the Establishment Clause.

Considerable current legal activity focuses on challenges to instruction about the origin of humanity. Despite two Supreme Court rulings striking down efforts to bar evolution or to require equal emphasis on the biblical account of creation in science classes, in more than half the states during the last decade, there has been political activity to attempt requiring the teaching of alternative theories to evolution. In 2004, a Pennsylvania federal court struck down a school district's policy instructing administrators to read a statement in 9th-grade biology classes that evolution is a theory. The statement also referred students to a book explaining Intelligent Design, which asserts there must be an intelligent designer because human beings are too complex to have evolved randomly by natural selection. The court reasoned that the policy was a ploy to put religious beliefs in the science curriculum.

Some controversies arose when students wanted to include sectarian materials in their presentations, artwork, or other school assignments. Schools have usually prevailed in denying such requests. For example, the Sixth Circuit upheld a school district's prohibition on an elementary school student showing in class a videotape of herself singing a proselytizing religious song. The court reasoned that student projects can be censored to ensure that the school is not viewed as endorsing religious content.

A sensitive current issue involves policies requiring instruction about tolerance based on race, sex, religion, and sexual orientation and barring harassment. Such policies have been challenged as impairing students' rights to express religious views, often those that condemn homosexuality. In 2006, the Ninth Circuit upheld school authorities who banned t-shirts with phrases degrading homosexuality (e.g., "Our School Embraced What God Has Condemned") because these interfered with the rights of others "in the most fundamental way." But other courts have upheld students' free speech right to convey such religious views in the absence of a disruption, even though the expression is quite hurtful to some classmates. This issue, which the Supreme Court has not yet [as of 2009] addressed, pits two important interests against each other—protecting the expression of private religious views and maintaining a civil and respectful school environment.

The Issue for Educators

Educators are expected to exercise sound judgment and follow well-established legal principles, and they can be liable for damages if they fail to do so. Ignorance of clearly established law is not a legitimate defense. Under the First Amendment's religion clauses, some activities are plainly prohibited, whereas others are protected. Educators need to know which activities are in each category. For example, Supreme Court precedent is well established that public schools cannot sponsor devotional activities (e.g., reading a prayer over the public address system) and teachers can't try to influence students' religious beliefs (e.g., posting religious materials in their classrooms). These activities could result in school district liability and dismissal of the employees involved. However, the Free Speech Clause protects private religious expression in public schools under certain circumstances, so educators must ensure that they aren't impairing students' rights to express private religious views or to distribute sectarian literature during noninstructional time. Yet, school personnel or outside groups can't distribute Bibles or other sectarian materials in public schools. Also, educators must not discriminate against student or community religious meetings if other groups are allowed to use school facilities when classes aren't in session.

Educators should adopt clear policies for reviewing challenges to the curriculum, and such policies should be enacted before a controversy arises. In addition, teachers should ensure that alternative instructional assignments are available to ease the burden on students' exercise of sincere religious beliefs and that expectations are explicit so that students are not faulted for using proselytizing materials where an assignment's purpose is ambiguous. Guidelines are available from the U.S. Department of Education and professional groups to assist educators in making informed decisions where the law is not clear.

Teachers often are hesitant to discuss church-state controversies with students for fear of being accused of promoting religion in violation of the Establishment Clause, but this is unfortunate. Teachers can and should provide instruction about religion and address the rationale for the First Amendment's religious guarantees. Educators can capitalize on students' requests to incorporate religious tenets in the classroom by providing instruction about constitutional guarantees and why certain activities aren't appropriate in public schools.

For activities that aren't banned under the Establishment Clause or required by the Free Speech or Free Exercise Clauses, school personnel have considerable discretion. It is important to remember that simply because a practice is constitutional does not mean that educators should promote it. To illustrate, the Supreme Court has rejected an Establishment Clause challenge to releasing students to receive religious instruction off school grounds during the school day. However, there may be other reasons to avoid this practice, such as ensuring that students of minority faiths do not feel uncomfortable and disadvantaged because they are placed in study hall when classmates leave for religious instruction. A preferable policy might be once a week to release all students an hour early so that they could participate in a range of activities.

Religious liberties deserve special protection in public schools because of the vulnerability of children. Educators' overriding concern should be to protect students from religious indoctrination by school personnel or classmates and to ensure that school policies don't unduly interfere with students' practice or expression of their beliefs. Balancing the competing interests can be daunting at times, but it is an important responsibility.

> *"It is necessary, even crucial, to follow the route of teaching about religion if we wish to maintain the principle of religious tolerance that undergirds the democratic republic."*

Schools Should Teach About Religion

Jeff Passe and Lara Willox

In the following viewpoint, Jeff Passe and Lara Willox argue that there is a need for public schools in the United States to teach about religion. Passe and Willox contend that the lack of knowledge of other religions has many negative consequences for society, even though it is largely accepted. They conclude that there is need for public support and teacher training to implement courses about religion. Passe is professor and chair of the Department of Secondary Education in the College of Education at Towson University in Maryland. Willox is assistant professor of early learning and childhood education at the University of West Georgia.

As you read, consider the following questions:

1. In what way do the authors claim that religion is not absent from classrooms?

2. Passe and Willox claim that the first public schools in the United States included what kind of religious instruction in their curricula?

3. The authors claim that scholars have suggested that Americans would support religion in public schools if what two conditions were met?

A mericans are confused about the role of religion in schools. On one hand, we have been taught about the separation of church and state. This concept is frequently misunderstood, as we shall see, but it guides the thinking of many educators who claim that principle as a reason to avoid the topic of religion entirely.

On the other hand, most educators accept that education about religion is essential to understanding the content of social studies. Indeed, it is instrumental in reaching one of the main goals of American schools: the development of active citizens. Without studying religion, how can a student possibly understand such topics as the Crusades; religious persecution; the formation of India and Pakistan; and the election of John F. Kennedy, America's first Catholic president—not to mention more recent events and controversies, such as 9/11; the Israeli-Palestinian dispute; the edicts of Pope Benedict; and the positions of the Christian right on abortion, gay rights, and stem cell research?

The Challenge of Teaching About Religion

The power of this content helps explain why almost every state and school district curriculum makes reference to increasing students' knowledge of world religions. The challenge is not getting such content into the curriculum; it is already there. The challenge is getting teachers to teach the content.

Religion is not absent from classrooms; because most teachers are accustomed to traditional approaches to community and school celebrations, religious subtexts often emerge. Teachers and schools engage in such activities as displaying Christmas decorations, singing traditional songs with religious connotations, and reciting sectarian prayers in the classroom.

To address the challenge of teaching about religion without proselytizing, we must explore the assumptions and causes underlying each set of factors in our national confusion over the role of religion in public schools. There is a way out. Although it may be disruptive, it is necessary, even crucial, to follow the route of teaching about religion if we wish to maintain the principle of religious tolerance that undergirds the democratic republic that has evolved for more than two hundred years.

The History of Religious Freedom

The U.S. Constitution explicitly addresses the relationship between church and state, forming the basis for further debate and guidelines on this issue. To understand the constitutional guidelines regarding the intersection of government and religion, we must consider the historical antecedents of the policies. By doing so, we are introducing the topic of religion into this article. We cannot teach history without teaching about religion any more than we could prepare beer without using yeast. Something crucial would be missing.

Many of the European groups that first settled in North America came to escape religious persecution. The best-known are the Pilgrims and Puritans who settled in Massachusetts because their refusal to conform to the Church of England made it impossible for them to remain in England. To practice their religion as they wished, they moved first to Holland and ultimately across the Atlantic to their new home at Plymouth. Quakers fled England for similar reasons, settling in Pennsylvania, and a group of English Catholics arrived in Maryland to exercise their own religious freedom.

Ironically, religious intolerance arose even among these first settlers, forcing Roger Williams to found a new colony in Rhode Island when the Puritan leaders of Massachusetts discriminated against those who shared his alternative views of God and religious practice. At the same time, Spanish settlers in the South and West were slaughtering Native Americans who refused to convert to Catholicism. When African slaves were brought to the New World, they too were deprived of their native religions, along with the rest of their freedoms.

During the colonial period in America, various philosophers argued against the concept of a state religion, viewing it as a dangerous practice that would limit individual freedom. This movement influenced our founders to create a constitution that was neutral with regard to religion. The word *neutral* is an important concept that will receive further elaboration.

Although the language of the original Constitution was neutral with regard to religion, the matter of religious freedom was not explicitly addressed until after the Philadelphia Constitutional Convention in 1787. Several colonies refused to endorse the new document unless it specifically protected various freedoms. In response, a group of leaders prepared the Bill of Rights, which comprised the first ten amendments to the Constitution. With the passage of the Bill of Rights, the term *freedom of religion* became the official policy of the new nation.

The Separation of Church and State

The First Amendment to the Constitution reads, "Congress shall make no law respecting an establishment of religion, or prohibiting the free exercise thereof." This "Establishment Clause" does not say anything about the teaching of religion, only that our government may not promote or endorse a religion, nor may it stop people from freely practicing their religion. Thus, we say that the state must be neutral with regard to religion.

When the Bill of Rights was written and when, in 1802, President Thomas Jefferson referred to a "wall of separation between church and state," there were no state-authorized public schools. Education was primarily the province of churches, which designated religious education as their foremost purpose.

Public schools as we know them today did not begin until the late 1800s, when, ironically, Massachusetts Protestants felt threatened by the influx of Irish immigrant children to the streets of Boston and sought to Americanize them through a public educational system, thereby avoiding the possible expansion of Roman Catholic schools.

The first public schools included religious instruction in the curriculum, instruction specifically designed to promote Protestant ways of thinking. Over time, a series of Supreme Court rulings applied the Establishment Clause to schools, thereby prohibiting schools from celebrating particular religions, or even from promoting religion over secular belief systems. Most schools discontinued the practice of public prayer, holiday celebrations with religious themes, and—taking matters to the extreme—teaching about religion altogether.

Churches, meanwhile, continued to offer parochial religious education. Many children went to church schools to learn about their own religions on Sundays or after school. Many others learned religion at home from their families. This pattern has remained constant.

The Absence of Religious Knowledge

Parents who preferred more intensive religious teaching sought out non-governmental schools. They objected to the absence of instruction in their own particular religious views. In other words, they wanted a merger of education and religion—as long as it included their own sectarian beliefs.

Parents seem comfortable with children knowing their own religions without venturing into the beliefs or practices of others. Their goal, after all, is usually indoctrination. Parents, understandably, want their children to be like themselves. They are not interested in having children make religious choices that differ from family traditions, based on the study of comparative religion. The absence of religion in public schools therefore seems to be just fine with the public.

One of the authors suffered personally from a lack of knowledge about religion. Although he excelled in social studies, he did not learn about world religions, or even American religions, in school. In his neighborhood, there were Catholics and Jews. He had heard of Protestants but did not know any. Needless to say, this gap in his education meant that he lacked a realistic view of the world. This handicapped him when he moved to the South, where Protestants dominate. He did not know the difference between a Baptist and a Methodist, a distinction that was important to his neighbors. He was also unprepared to study current events that required an understanding of the quarrels between various religious groups. We shudder to hear acquaintances make ill-informed statements about other religions, but we cannot blame them. They were never taught the content.

The Rise of Multicultural Education

The gap in religious knowledge has become more serious in recent years because of changing patterns of integration in the United States, a situation that is also being experienced throughout Europe. The newest pattern is the growing presence of cultures that do not conform to the Judeo-Christian religious tradition that previously characterized the vast majority of Americans. In the past in this nation of immigrants, Americans were somewhat more likely to accept the arrival of Italians, Poles, Puerto Ricans, Scandinavians, and Russians, because the newcomers engaged in similar religious practices.

Of course, there have always been small segments with other beliefs in this country, including Hindus, Muslims, Native Americans, and others, but these groups tended to avoid confrontation. This tendency was helped by housing patterns in which members of religious groups were likely to live in the same areas. Thus, in areas like urban Chinatowns, Indian reservations, and heavily Jewish suburbs, the minority groups dominated the schools, which enabled them to ignore the dominant religious

Religious Knowledge in the United States

The Pew Forum's [2010] religious knowledge survey included 32 questions about various aspects of religion: the Bible, Christianity, Judaism, Mormonism, world religions, religion in public life, and atheism and agnosticism. The average respondent answered 16 [50%] of the 32 religious knowledge questions correctly. Just 2% of those surveyed answered 29 [90%] or more questions correctly (including just eight individuals, out of 3,412 surveyed, who scored a perfect 32); 3% correctly answered fewer than five questions (including six respondents who answered no questions correctly).

The scores on individual questions ranged from 8% to 89% correct. At the top end of that scale, at least eight-in-ten Americans know that teachers are not allowed to lead public school classes in prayer, that the term "atheist" refers to someone who does not believe in God, and that Mother Teresa was Catholic. At the other end of the spectrum, just 8% know that the 12th-century philosopher and Torah scholar Maimonides was Jewish, and 11% correctly identify Jonathan Edwards, viewed by many scholars as the pre-eminent American theologian, as a preacher during the First Great Awakening, a period of heightened religious fervor in the 1730s and '40s.

Pew Research Center, Forum on Religion and Public Life, May 19–June 6, 2010.

customs practiced outside their enclaves and integrate their own religious customs in the schools.

The segregated housing patterns held for the flood of Asian immigrants in the 1980s. Despite the major increase in Japanese,

Chinese, Vietnamese, Filipino, and Asian Indian populations, these groups, following previous patterns, settled in relatively homogenous neighborhoods. Unlike their predecessors, however, these immigrants' numbers were not large enough to dominate nearby schools. Because Hindu and Buddhist practices were so unfamiliar to the majority of Judeo-Christian Americans, a call was made by leading social studies educators to endorse the newly developed movement for "multicultural education." One of the purposes of this movement was to insure that students would learn about not only their own cultures, but also those of others.

The relatively neutral word *culture* includes religion but also food, dress, language, arts, and everyday customs of behavior. Most educators who endorsed or implemented multicultural education would tiptoe around or ignore any in-depth study of religion.

American Knowledge of Islam

The issue of religious knowledge reached the forefront after 9/11, when Americans began to recognize how little they knew about Islam. Europeans have been wrestling with that same realization for decades, as they have experienced large influxes of North African and Turkish immigrants into their once relatively homogenous cultures.

A series of events following 9/11 demonstrated American ignorance of religion. We saw Hindus and Sikhs, mistakenly identified as Muslims, experience discrimination and worse. We heard jokes that ridiculed Islam or generalized about the entire religion on the basis of the conduct of a small group of terrorists. Xenophobia and intolerance abounded.

American society has taken commendable steps to alleviate these situations and provide some remedial education for society at large, including sensitive media coverage. Yet these steps are insufficient. They are not focused on the school curriculum and are neither systematic nor comprehensive.

The Need for Public Support

The challenge of meeting Americans' needs to understand their own and their neighbors' religions involves both auricular and instructional adjustments, all of which disrupt the status quo. The curriculum must focus more on cultural anthropology, with a special emphasis on comparative religion. This policy change cannot occur without substantial public support. Unfortunately, currents today are moving in the opposite direction. Social studies, which includes anthropology, is gradually disappearing from the elementary and middle school curriculum in favor of literacy and mathematics. Elementary teachers are skipping the topic altogether, and middle school teachers who teach social studies as part of a block are increasingly likely to de-emphasize social studies goals. This is primarily a result of the No Child Left Behind legislation, which appears to be narrowing the curriculum. Secondary school social studies, which is set by time periods and not influenced by No Child Left Behind, does not suffer from a loss of teaching time for the subject but is affected by the emphasis on high-stakes, end-of-grade tests. These tests, which tend to control what is taught and emphasized, seldom include questions related to anthropology or religious knowledge.

To put the matter in a humorous perspective, it is like the old joke about how many psychologists it takes to change a light bulb. The answer is, "Just one, but the light bulb has to want to change." In this case, our society must accept that our citizens' lack of knowledge about religion is unacceptable. This can only happen with a major campaign that communicates the benefits of religious knowledge in promoting better relations with the Muslims in the next house, the Hindu in the marketplace, the Greek Orthodox coworker, the Seventh-Day Adventist in the next state, or the legions of religious sects everywhere.

We will not offer a treatise on globalization. The ease of interacting with others around the world has become apparent. Yet our society must be alerted to the social upheaval that accompanies globalization. These changes must be presented honestly, with both positive and negative consequences. Many scholars believe that the American public would support greater emphasis on religion in the curriculum if (1) it can be presented as a way to promote harmony, peace, and economic progress and (2) it can be accomplished fairly, without indoctrination.

The Need for Teacher Training

This brings us to a different curricular challenge, which is much more daunting. Most teachers lack the knowledge to teach about world religions. Indeed, teachers' lack of a firm foundation regarding comparative religion has been proposed as one of the main obstacles in overcoming their tendency to avoid the topic.

To make matters worse, American teachers also lack the skills required to teach the content appropriately. A single preservice course in social studies methods is insufficient for teachers to develop instructional techniques that promote tolerance, sensitivity, nonjudgmental expression of beliefs, and an in-depth grasp of the nuances of major world religions. This is especially true for elementary teachers, who are increasingly likely to have gaps in their knowledge of basic social studies, let alone cultural anthropology.

Thus, American schools are not ready to teach religion. It would be the blind leading the blind, resulting in the transmission of bias, misconceptions, and harmful stereotypes. A single in-service workshop will not suffice. Teachers will require a comprehensive training program that relies heavily on the development of high-quality curriculum materials, both for teacher training and for use in the pre-K–12 classroom. Such a program will demand a large investment by governments and possibly foundations as well.

Once the proper professional development opportunities are offered, their implementation must be strongly supported by administrators. This effort must be clearly communicated to parents and other citizens, and communications should stress that the schools are teaching *about* religion, not teaching children what to believe. It is to be expected that some parents fear indoctrination and need to be reassured. It is also to be expected that a minority of parents and citizens object to any presentation about religion that does not promote their particular viewpoints. Such reactions must be recognized as those of a small minority as we promote the benefits of a religious education curriculum.

As for curricular materials, excellent nonbiased methods and materials already exist. If there were a greater demand for them, the supply would increase. It all comes down to developing that demand.

| *"The broader encroachment of the anti-religious judiciary . . . has taken place below the radar of most Americans."*

Anti-Religious Speech Police in America

Newt Gingrich

In the following viewpoint, Newt Gingrich argues that recent events show that the judiciary in America has become too powerful and is using its power to advance an antireligious agenda. He claims that the Founding Fathers of the United States never intended for judges to have such power. Gingrich contends that judges who attempt to remove all religion from the public sphere are out of touch with Americans and should be removed from their positions. Gingrich is a former Speaker of the US House of Representatives and the author of Rediscovering God in America: Reflections on the Role of Faith in Our Nation's History and Future.

As you read, consider the following questions:

1. Which federal district judge issued an order to stop a school's valedictorian from saying a prayer as part of her graduation speech, according to Gingrich?

Newt Gingrich, "Anti-Religious Speech Police in America," *Human Events*, June 22, 2011.

2. According to Gingrich, how did President Thomas Jefferson deal with out-of-control federal judges?
3. Who has final power in America, according to the author?

C an you imagine high school administrators being threatened with jail if their students said any of the following words? "Prayer," "stand," "bow your heads," or "amen"?

Can you imagine a graduation ceremony in which the word "invocation" was replaced with "opening remarks" and "benediction" was replaced with "closing remarks"—by order of a federal judge? Or a judge declaring that such an order would be "enforced by incarceration or other sanctions for contempt of Court if not obeyed?"

This sounds like a scenario that might occur under a dictatorship, but it happened earlier this month in the Medina Valley Independent School District near San Antonio, Texas. It is just one recent example of how anti-religious many on the Left have become.

It is bad enough that NBC revealed its anti-religious bias by editing out "under God" from the Pledge of Allegiance last weekend.

It is bad enough that President Obama has skipped the phrase "our Creator" at least four times when citing the Declaration of Independence, even when the teleprompter read that we are "endowed by our Creator."

At least neither NBC nor President Obama threatened to put anyone in jail.

Federal District Judge Fred Biery issued the order to stop the school's valedictorian from saying a prayer as part of her graduation speech. He did so in the name of the First Amendment, which is supposed to prevent government prohibitions of the free exercise of religion and protect the freedom of speech.

Judge Biery's decision clearly is not about defending the Constitution. It is the anti-religious judicial thought police at work here in America.

It is time for Americans who are fed up with this kind of repression by an anti-religious judiciary to act decisively. Judge Biery's decision is so outrageous that the American people should not accept his continued employment on the federal bench.

The Federalist Papers and a Limited Judicial Branch

The Founders never intended for judges to have free rein to interpret the Constitution according to their own ideological purposes. In fact, Alexander Hamilton is quite clear in the *Federalist No. 78* that judges who conduct themselves like Biery will have short tenures.

"The judiciary," Hamilton writes, ". . . will always be the least dangerous to the political rights of the Constitution, because it will be least in capacity to annoy or injure them." Among the three co-equal branches of government (each of which is charged with interpreting and upholding the Constitution), he writes that the judiciary "can never attack with success either of the other two."

Hamilton's description of a judiciary subordinate in power to the president and the Congress is a long way from the modern doctrine of judicial supremacy, by which the judiciary has asserted itself as the supreme authority for Constitutional interpretation.

By Hamilton's standard, at least, Judge Biery has clearly failed to avoid the kind of offenses that should rightly provoke attacks by the legislative and executive branches.

In the Hamiltonian spirit, then, I would like to offer a simple solution to the problem.

Judge Biery, Meet Thomas Jefferson

President Thomas Jefferson—who, together with his Secretary of State James Madison, knew more than a little about the Constitution—had a solution for dealing with out-of-control federal judges: he abolished the judgeships of 18 out of 35 of them.

That's right. In the Judiciary Act of 1802, Jefferson eliminated more than half the sitting federal judges.

As a first step toward reining in an out-of-control, anti-religious bigotry on the bench, let's start with this modest suggestion: *Judge Biery's office should be abolished by Congress.* He should go home.

The American people would be better off without a judge whose anti-religious extremism leads him to ban a high school valedictorian from saying even the word "prayer."

A Nation Like No Other

In my new book, *A Nation Like No Other: Why American Exceptionalism Matters,* I discuss the basis of Jefferson's concern about the judiciary, and especially about its claim to supremacy as "the ultimate arbiter of all constitutional questions." The idea that unelected and unaccountable judges would dictate to the people the meaning of the Constitution, he wrote in an 1820 letter to William Jarvis, was "a very dangerous doctrine indeed, and one which would place us under the despotism of an oligarchy."

Jefferson was adamant that the Constitution had not established a "single tribunal" to interpret its meaning specifically because the Founders understood that any group to whom alone that power was confided "would become despots."

Instead, the branches of government were created to be co-equal, each itself charged with interpreting the Constitution and "responsible to the people in [its] elective capacity."

"The exemption of the judges from that [accountability] is quite dangerous enough," Jefferson wrote. "I know of no safe depository of the ultimate powers of society, but the people themselves."

This challenge to judicial supremacy is intimately connected to the heart of what makes America exceptional. As I write in *A Nation Like No Other,* the final power in America lies not with judges or presidents or bureaucrats, but with the American people. We loan power to the government. And as Jefferson demonstrated dramatically when he abolished eighteen federal judgeships, we can take it back when it is abused.

Few things exhibit the danger of judicial abuse more clearly than when judges like Biery use their positions to advance agendas so far out of the mainstream that they end up dictating word choice at a local high school graduation.

In Biery's case, the order was so extreme that thankfully it was stayed by the appeals court just hours before the graduation.

The broader encroachment of the anti-religious judiciary, however, has taken place below the radar of most Americans. It has proceeded, as Jefferson wrote of the branch in another letter, "like gravity, ever acting, with noiseless foot, unalarming advance, gaining ground step by step, and holding what it gains . . . engulfing insidiously the special governments into the jaws of that which feeds them."

Thomas Jefferson was right. When judges are policing graduation speeches for religious content, the judiciary has clearly advanced too far. It is time for the American people to reassert their authority.

They can start in the U.S. District Court for Western Texas.

Your Friend,

Newt Gingrich

P.S.—The Actual Order

Just so no one will think I have exaggerated the outrageousness of Judge Biery's attack on free speech, here is his order:

SIGNED this 1st day of June, 2011.

Accordingly, it is hereby ORDERED that the Medina Valley Independent School District and its officials, agents, servants, and employees, as well as all persons acting in concert with them, are prohibited from allowing a prayer (as defined in paragraph (b) below) to be included in the June 4, 2011 graduation ceremony for Medina Valley High School. More specifically:

a. The district was to remove the terms "invocation" and "benediction" from the program of ceremonies. The terms shall be replaced with "opening remarks" and "closing remarks".

b. The district, through its officials, shall instruct the students previously selected to deliver the invocation and benediction to modify their remarks to be statements of their own beliefs as opposed to leading the audience in prayer. These students, and all other persons scheduled to speak during the graduation ceremony, shall be instructed not to present a prayer, to with, they shall be instructed that they may not ask audience members to "stand", "join in prayer", or "bow their heads," they may not end their remarks with "amen" or "in a [deity's name] we pray," and they shall not otherwise deliver a message that would commonly be understood to be a prayer, nor use the word "prayer". The students may in stating their own personal beliefs speak through conduct such as kneeling to face Mecca, the wearing of a yarmulke or hijab or making the sign of the cross.

c. The District, through its officials, shall review, and many any necessary changes to, the students' revised remarks to ensure that those remarks comply with this Order, and shall instruct the students that they must not deviate from the approved remarks in making their presentations.

Because this suit seeks to enforce fundamental constitutional norms, it is further ORDERED that the security requirements of Federal Rule of Civil Procedure 65 (c) is waived, and that this injunctive order shall be effective immediately and shall be enforced by incarceration or other sanctions for contempt of Court if not obeyed by District officials and their agents.

"*Church-state separation is not a matter of oppression for any religious group, but a means of ensuring that all religious views enjoy a level playing field.*"

Government Neutrality on Religion Is Not Antireligion

David Niose

In the following viewpoint, David Niose argues that government should be neutral toward religion and that, contrary to criticism from many believers, such a stance does not constitute an antireligion bias. Niose gives a series of examples in which he contends that antireligion bias exists not when government refrains from any endorsement of religion but, rather, where government actively condemns religion. Based on his examples, Niose concludes that anything less than government neutrality toward religion is unfair. Niose is an attorney, president of the American Humanist Association, and author of Nonbeliever Nation: The Rise of Secular Americans.

As you read, consider the following questions:

1. According to the author, what would real antireligion bias look like with respect to school prayer?

2. According to the author, what would real antireligion bias look like with respect to the national motto?
3. Niose claims that when the Religious Right complains about neutrality it demonstrates what?

One of the hallmarks of the Religious Right is its consistent inability to understand the concept of government neutrality on religion. In its eyes virtually all institutions, especially those governmental, are assessed as either "for" or "against" God, with the middle ground of neutrality not an option.

This poses a problem for Secular Americans, who generally don't seek a government that is anti-religion, only one that is neutral. Unfortunately, whenever secular groups or individuals attempt to encourage governmental religious neutrality, predictable cries will be heard from the Christian Right that religion and God are "under attack." The proposed neutrality is seen as yet more proof that never has a majority population been so oppressed as America's Christians.

Neutrality and Bias in Public Schools

Therefore, in an attempt to illustrate the difference between government *neutrality on religion* and government *bias against religion*, the list below examines several popular church-state issues from both perspectives—neutrality and anti-religion bias. Bear in mind that nobody is suggesting that government should actually reflect an anti-religion bias, but the examples are provided in order to show what such bias might look like. Here they are:

The neutral action: Prohibiting school-sponsored religious instruction in public schools, whether in the form of Bible instruction, "creation science," or any other means of injecting God or religion into public school curricula.

What real anti-religion bias would look like: If schools affirmatively taught that there is no God, that all theistic religion is wrong, then the Religious Right would have a valid claim that schools are "anti-religion."

The neutral action: Prohibiting public schools from sponsoring any kind of prayer exercises. (Contrary to popular myth this does not stop individuals from praying on their own free time, because it only prohibits government sponsorship of such exercises. As such, alarmist cries that "God has been kicked out of schools" are entirely overblown.)

What real anti-religion bias would look like: If schools prohibited children from praying on their own, even during their own free time in a manner not obstructing others, that would be "anti-religion."

Neutrality and Bias in Government Endorsement

The neutral action: Removing "under God" from the Pledge of Allegiance to the Flag, returning to the original wording of ". . . one nation indivisible, with liberty and justice for all."

What real anti-religion would look like: Rather than just remove the "under God" wording, a truly anti-religion government would insert wording that would make an affirmative anti-religion statement, such as "one nation, godless, indivisible, with liberty and justice for all." As outlandish as this seems to believers, the current pro-God version seems just as inappropriate to many nonbelievers. This shows the wisdom of simple neutrality, where nobody's beliefs are disrespected.

The neutral action: Ending government sponsorship of the National Day of Prayer, an annual event that was created in modern times by religious conservatives for the primary purpose of pushing a religious agenda into the public sphere. A National Day of Prayer that is sponsored by various churches, rather than the government, would be fine, but secular citizens (and many religious citizens as well) don't like their government sponsoring a religious event like an annual day of prayer.

What real anti-religion would look like: An anti-religion government would sponsor a National Day of Blasphemy. In fact, a day in recognition of blasphemy, though not government-sponsored, already exists. Every September 30 infidels of all stripes from around the world celebrate Blasphemy Day, a day that recognizes and appreciates free speech and the freedom to criticize religion.

The neutral action: Scrapping the clearly religious national motto that was adopted in 1956, "In God We Trust," and returning to the excellent motto crafted by the founders, "E Pluribus Unum" (meaning "Out of many, one").

What real anti-religion would look like: There are many ways that a government could declare truly anti-religious sentiments. A motto such as "In God We Don't Trust," for example, would be unambiguous in this regard.

The Value of Church-State Separation

The neutral action: Ending the practice of sending tax dollars to churches in the name of "faith-based partnerships." Every year millions of tax dollars are funneled to churches for social programs and similar purposes. In practice there is little oversight, even though the money is not supposed to be used for proselytizing or any other religious purpose. The religious organizations are not even subject to the discrimination laws that nonreligious entities must follow. These programs are often taxpayer-funded cash cows for religious organizations.

What real anti-religion bias would look like: If government were truly anti-religious it would not only not funnel money to churches, but it would impose a special tax on religion, forcing religious organizations to funnel money to the federal and state treasuries.

These examples show us that church-state separation is not a matter of oppression for any religious group, but a means of ensuring that all religious views enjoy a level playing field. When the Religious Right complains about such fairness and neutrality, it only demonstrates that it expects special treatment for its views, and that anything less will be seen as unfair.

Interestingly, when religious conservatives claim that "majority rule" should allow a pro-religion bias, one must wonder whether they would concede that, should nonbelievers ever attain a majority in America (a plausible hypothesis given general trends), this would justify an anti-religion bias such as that described in the samples above. Probably not. And this demonstrates why all sides should agree that neutrality should be the goal regardless of who is in the majority.

Periodical and Internet Sources Bibliography

The following articles have been selected to supplement the diverse views presented in this chapter.

Americans United for Separation of Church and State	"Praying for Legal Behavior: Why Teachers Should Not Be Preachers," *Church & State*, October 2010.
John A. Coleman	"One Nation Under God: Can We Please Both Church and State in a Pluralistic Society?," *America*, March 12, 2012.
Allen D. Hertzke	"The Supreme Court and Religious Liberty," *Weekly Standard*, October 18, 2010.
Eliza Krigman	"The Bible Goes to School," *National Journal*, March 19, 2010.
Dennis Prager	"Secular Fanatics," *FrontPage*, February 2, 2012. www.frontpagemag.com.
Stephen Prothero	"It's Time to Teach Religion in Schools," *USA Today*, October 3, 2010.
Alex Rose	"How About a 'Freedom from Religion' in the First Amendment?," *Providence (RI) Journal*, February 3, 2010.
Jeffrey Rosen	"High Stakes for Church and State Separation," *Moment*, January–February 2012.
Katherine Stewart	"Separation of Church and School," *New York Times*, June 12, 2011.
Fay Voshell	"A Forced Marriage of Church and State," *American Thinker*, February 26, 2012. www.americanthinker.com.
Kurt Williamsen	"The Ruling Religion in Schools," *New American*, January 9, 2012.

OPPOSING
VIEWPOINTS®
SERIES

CHAPTER 3

Is the Right to Due Process in Danger?

Chapter Preface

The right to due process of law is guaranteed by both the Fifth and Fourteenth Amendments to the US Constitution. The Fifth Amendment states, "No person shall . . . be deprived of life, liberty, or property, without due process of law," a restriction on the actions of the federal government; whereas the Fourteenth Amendment is applicable to actions of state governments, demanding that they also not "deprive any person of life, liberty, or property, without due process of law." The right to due process protects individuals from arbitrary and unjust actions of government that infringe upon individual liberties. The right to procedural due process, the oldest understanding of the right to due process, demands that government follow certain procedures before depriving anyone of life, liberty, or property. But a more recent, and more controversial, understanding of due process that includes the right to substantive due process makes certain deprivations—such as depriving an individual of the right to privacy—unconstitutional no matter what the process. This chapter focuses on the right to procedural due process.

The right to procedural due process covers any government proceedings that may deprive an individual of life, liberty, or property. Over the last few decades, the US Supreme Court has extended most of the criminal procedural guarantees of the Bill of Rights to the states—meaning state governments are held to the same standards as the federal government—along with other policies that uphold the doctrine of fundamental fairness, a concept that was first articulated by the Court in the 1932 case of *Powell v. Alabama*. That case found that a defendant in a capital trial—one involving the death penalty—must be given access to an attorney. The right to procedural due process is, in essence, the right to fair trial procedures before the government may impose the death penalty, sentence imprisonment, or seize any property.

The right to due process identified in both the Fifth and Fourteenth Amendments explicitly refers to all people without regard to their citizenship. Thus, the right to due process is afforded to any person in the United States when faced with possible deprivation of life, liberty, or property. There is much debate today, however, about how due process rights ought to be interpreted for persons held during wartime or for persons who are in the United States illegally. In this chapter, opposing viewpoints are explored on the issue of due process rights for terrorists overseas, terrorist suspects held on US soil (including Guantánamo Bay, Cuba), and illegal immigrants within the United States.

> "Section 1021 [of the National Defense Authorization Act] reaffirms the military's legal position on holding Guantanamo detainees who pose a threat to the United States."

The Military Should Be Allowed to Detain Noncitizen Terrorist Suspects

Charles D. Stimson

In the following viewpoint, Charles D. Stimson argues that the US government was correct to codify the ability of the military to detain enemies without trial for the duration of the war on terror. Stimson claims that section 1021 of the 2012 National Defense Authorization Act only allows noncitizens to be prosecuted by military commission and therefore does not violate the constitutional rights of US citizens. Stimson is the chief of staff and a senior legal fellow at the Heritage Foundation in Washington, DC.

As you read, consider the following questions:

1. According to Stimson, which persons are allowed to be detained under section 1021 of the 2012 National Defense Authorization Act?

Charles D. Stimson, "The National Defense Authorization Act and Military Detention of US Citizens," *WebMemo*, no. 3497, February 10, 2012, pp. 1–3. Copyright © 2012 by The Heritage Foundation. All rights reserved. Reproduced by permission.

2. What is the primary statutory authority for the war against terrorism, according to the author?
3. According to Stimson, why was section 1021 of the 2012 National Defense Authorization Act necessary?

For the 50th consecutive year, the National Defense Authorization Act (NDAA) for Fiscal Year 2012 provides funding and authorities for the U.S. military. It also includes several policy provisions regarding the handling of al-Qaeda and Taliban terrorists. Although we have previously expressed concerns regarding NDAA provisions relating to transfer restrictions for foreign detainees held at Guantanamo [Bay, a U.S. naval base in Cuba], section 1021 of the NDAA contains important and constructive language that strengthens America's continuing fight against terrorists. Some organizations and individuals have criticized section 1021, and some have claimed that this bill creates or expands federal authority to detain U.S. citizens indefinitely and without due process. Those claims are false.

The Detention of U.S. Citizens

The NDAA has not impacted the conditions under which a U.S. citizen may (or may not) be detained. In fact, section 1021 of the NDAA is explicit: The law regarding how U.S. citizens are handled, including the right to *habeas corpus* [the right to seek judicial review of one's imprisonment], is the same today as it was the day before it was passed.

In order to understand fully why section 1021 does not create or expand authority to detain U.S. citizens, it is important to review briefly some important concepts, statutes, and case law.

Section 1021 of the NDAA states that *"[n]othing in this section shall be construed to affect existing law or authorities relating to the detention of United States citizens, lawful resident aliens of the United States, or any other persons who are captured or arrested in the United States."*

The Covered Persons

Section 1021 also defines the universe of persons covered under the section and defines the universe of dispositions available to the government for each detainee.

Under the NDAA, covered persons include: (1) A person who planned, authorized, committed, or aided the terrorist attacks that occurred on September 11, 2001, or harbored those responsible for those attacks, and; (2) A person who was a part of or substantially supported al-Qaeda, the Taliban, or associated forces that are engaged in hostilities against the United States or its coalition partners, including any person who has committed a belligerent act or has directly supported such hostilities in aid of such enemy forces.

Under the law of armed conflict or the law of war, a nation engaged in armed conflict has the legal authority to detain enemies who have engaged in combatant actions, including acts of belligerence, until the end of hostilities. A nation, including the United States, may detain captured enemy fighters—not as punishment, but to keep them from returning to the battlefield. The law of war does not differentiate or discriminate between enemy combatants who are citizens or non-citizens. History is replete with examples of citizens who became members of the opposing forces and were subject to detention when captured. These time-honored and humane principles existed prior to 9/11, after 9/11, and were the state of the law prior to the passage of the NDAA.

As for the notion that the NDAA allows for U.S. citizens to be prosecuted under the Military Commissions Act of 2009, the Act applies only to "alien unprivileged enemy belligerents." "Aliens" under the Act means non-citizens, and thus the Act does not allow for prosecution of U.S. citizens by military commission.

The War Against Terrorism

The primary statutory authority for the war against terrorism is the September 18, 2001, congressional "Authorization for Use of Military Force" (AUMF). It authorizes the President to use "all necessary and appropriate force against those nations, organizations, or persons he determines planned, authorized, committed, or aided the terrorist attacks that occurred on September 11, 2001." And although the AUMF language does not specifically include the word "detain" or "detention," lawmakers, policymakers, the [George W.] Bush and [Barack] Obama Administrations, and the courts have all interpreted the AUMF to necessarily include the ability to detain the enemy for the duration of hostilities.

In 2004, the U.S. Supreme Court held in *Hamdi v. Rumsfeld* that the AUMF provides authority for the military to detain a U.S. citizen captured overseas on the battlefield in Afghanistan on U.S. soil until the end of hostilities. However, the controlling plurality of the Court explicitly noted that "[a]ll agree that absent suspension, the writ of habeas corpus remains available to every individual detained within the United States." The plurality further noted that "[a]ll agree suspension of the writ has not occurred here." Thus, the writ of habeas corpus remains available to any individual detained in the United States.

Not only is habeas corpus review available to both citizens and non-citizens detained in the United States, but the Supreme Court has also extended the privilege to foreign detainees held at the U.S. Naval Station in Guantanamo Bay, Cuba. U.S. military and national security professionals have been litigating Guantanamo detainee habeas cases for several years. Section 1021 reaffirms the military's legal position on holding Guantanamo detainees who pose a threat to the United States. The Department of Justice is already citing section 1021 in its legal briefs to support the military's detention of foreign terrorists held at Guantanamo, as well as in Afghanistan.

The Need for Authority to Detain

So, why was section 1021 necessary, since it does not seem to change the status quo?

Despite the fact that the U.S. is drawing down its forces in Afghanistan, the enemy continues to engage in armed conflict against the United States and its allies. As the U.S. draws down forces, there is a legitimate concern that American courts may begin to chip away at the military's legal authority to detain al-Qaeda terrorists. Section 1021 essentially codifies the same detention language used by both the Bush and Obama Administrations that has been upheld by federal courts. Ten years after passage of the AUMF, this helps ensure that the military continues to have the authority to hunt down and detain al-Qaeda terrorists wherever they may hide.

In summary, the NDAA detainee provisions do not create or expand the government's ability to detain U.S. citizens. In no way does the NDAA negatively impact or change the constitutional rights of U.S. citizens. Instead, section 1021 strengthens the military's authority to detain individuals who are members of or substantially supporting al-Qaeda, the Taliban, and associated forces.

Misinformation regarding the impact of section 1021 should not detract from this significant step toward reinforcing the legal underpinnings of the war against terrorists.

> *"There is simply no question that [the National Defense Authorization Act] . . . significantly expands the statutory definitions of the War on Terror and those who can be targeted as part of it."*

The Military Should Not Be Allowed Indefinite Detention of Terrorist Suspects

Glenn Greenwald

In the following viewpoint, Glenn Greenwald argues that the 2012 National Defense Authorization Act entrenches the power of government to detain both citizens and noncitizens without trial for the duration of the War on Terror, while expanding the definition of the war. He claims that there are three myths spread by supporters of the bill to minimize concern about the new codification. Greenwald is a lawyer, a columnist, and the author of With Liberty and Justice for Some: How the Law Is Used to Destroy Equality and Protect the Powerful.

As you read, consider the following questions:

1. According to the author, section 1021 of the 2012 National Defense Authorization Act governs what resolution from 2001?

2. What component of section 1021 concerning covered persons is brand new, according to Greenwald?

3. According to the author, what is the only provision for which US citizens are exempted from the powers delineated by section 1021?

Condemnation of President [Barack] Obama is intense, and growing, as a result of his announced intent to sign into law the indefinite detention bill embedded in the 2012 National Defense Authorization Act (NDAA). These denunciations come not only from the nation's leading civil liberties and human rights groups, but also from the pro-Obama *New York Times* Editorial Page, which today [December 16, 2011,] has a scathing Editorial describing Obama's stance as "a complete political cave-in, one that reinforces the impression of a fumbling presidency" and lamenting that "the bill has so many other objectionable aspects that we can't go into them all," as well as from vocal Obama supporters such as [journalist] Andrew Sullivan, who wrote yesterday that this episode is "another sign that his campaign pledge to be vigilant about civil liberties in the war on terror was a lie." In damage control mode, White-House-allied groups are now trying to ride to the rescue with attacks on the ACLU [American Civil Liberties Union] and dismissive belittling of the bill's dangers.

For that reason, it is very worthwhile to briefly examine—and debunk—the three principal myths being spread by supporters of this bill, and to do so very simply: by citing the relevant provisions of the bill, as well as the relevant passages of the original 2001 Authorization to Use Military Force (AUMF), so that everyone can judge for themselves what this bill actually includes. . . .

Myth #1: This Bill Does Not Codify Indefinite Detention

Section 1021 of the NDAA governs, as its title says, "Authority of the Armed Forces to Detain Covered Persons Pursuant to the

AUMF." The first provision—section (a)—explicitly "affirms that the authority of the President" under the AUMF "includes the authority for the *Armed Forces of the United States to detain* covered persons." The next section, (b), defines "covered persons"— i.e., those who can be detained by the U.S. military—as "a person who was a part of or substantially supported al-Qaeda, the Taliban, or associated forces that are engaged in hostilities against the United States or its coalition partners." With regard to those "covered individuals," this is the power vested in the President by the next section, (c):

> (e) *Disposition Under Law of War.*—The disposition of a person under the law of war as described in subsection (a) may include the following:
>
> 1. Detention under the law of war *without trial until the end of the hostilities* authorized by the Authorization for Use of Military Force.

It simply cannot be any clearer within the confines of the English language that this bill codifies the power of indefinite detention. It expressly empowers the President—with regard to anyone *accused* of the acts in the section—to detain them "*without trial* until the end of the hostilities." That is the very definition of "indefinite detention," and the statute could not be clearer that it vests this power. Anyone claiming this bill does not codify indefinite detention should be forced to explain how they can claim that in light of this crystal clear provision.

It is true, as I've pointed out repeatedly, that both the [George W.] Bush and Obama administrations have argued that the 2001 AUMF *implicitly* (i.e., silently) already vests the power of indefinite detention in the President, and post-9/11 deferential courts have largely accepted that view (just as the Bush DOJ [Department of Justice] argued that the 2001 AUMF *implicitly* (i.e., silently) allowed them to eavesdrop on Americans without the warrants required by law). That's why the NDAA can state that nothing is intended to expand the 2001 AUMF while achieving exactly that: because the executive and judicial interpretation being given to the 2001 AUMF is already so much broader than its language provides.

But this is the first time this power of indefinite detention is being expressly codified by statute (there's not a word about detention powers in the 2001 AUMF). Indeed, as the ACLU and HRW [Human Rights Watch] both pointed out, it's the first time such powers are being codified in a statute since the [Joe] McCarthy era Internal Security Act of 1950. . . .

Myth #2: The Bill Does Not Expand the Scope of the War on Terror

This myth is very easily dispensed with. The scope of the war as defined by the original 2001 AUMF was, at least relative to this new bill, quite specific and narrow. Here's the full extent of the power the original AUMF granted:

> (a) *In general*—That the President is authorized to use all necessary and appropriate force against those nations, organizations, or persons he determines *planned, authorized, committed, or aided the terrorist attacks that occurred on September 11, 2001*, or harbored such organizations or persons, in order to prevent any future acts of international terrorism against the United States by such nations, organizations or persons.

Under the clear language of the 2001 AUMF, the President's authorization to use force was explicitly confined to those who (a) helped perpetrate the 9/11 attack or (b) harbored the perpetrators. That's it. Now look at how much broader the NDAA is with regard to who can be targeted:

> (b) *Covered Persons.*—A covered person under this section is any person as follows:
>
> 1. A person who planned, authorized, committed, or aided the terrorist attacks that occurred on

September 11, 2001, or harbored those responsible for those attacks.

2. A person who was a part of or *substantially supported* al-Qaeda, the Taliban, or *associated forces* that are engaged in hostilities against the United States or its coalition partners, including any person who has committed a belligerent act or has directly supported such hostilities in aid of such enemy forces.

Section (1) is basically a re-statement of the 2001 AUMF. But Section (2) is a brand new addition. It allows the President to target not only those who helped perpetrate the 9/11 attacks or those who harbored them, but also: anyone who "*substantially supports*" such groups *and/or* "associated forces." Those are extremely vague terms subject to wild and obvious levels of abuse. . . . This is a substantial statutory escalation of the War on Terror and the President's powers under it, and it occurs more than ten years after 9/11, with Osama bin Laden dead, and with the U.S. Government boasting that virtually all Al Qaeda leaders have been eliminated and the original organization (the one accused of perpetrating 9/11 attack) rendered inoperable.

It is true that both the Bush and Obama administrations have long been arguing that the original AUMF should be broadly "interpreted" so as to authorize force against this much larger scope of individuals, despite the complete absence of such language in that original AUMF. That's how the Obama administration justifies its ongoing bombing of Yemen and Somalia and its killing of people based on the claim that they support groups *that did not even exist at the time of 9/11*—i.e., they argue: *these new post-9/11 groups we're targeting are "associated forces" of Al Qaeda and the individuals we're killing "substantially support" those groups.* But this is the first time that Congress has codified that wildly expanded definition of the Enemy in the War on Terror. And all anyone has to do to see that is compare the old AUMF with the new one in the NDAA.

Myth #3: US Citizens Are Exempted from This New Bill

This is simply false, at least when expressed so definitively and without caveats. The bill is purposely muddled on this issue, which is what is enabling the falsehood.

There are two separate indefinite military detention provisions in this bill. The first, Section 1021, authorizes indefinite detention for the broad definition of "covered persons" discussed above in the prior point. And that section does provide that "Nothing *in this section* shall be construed to affect existing law or authorities relating to the detention of United States citizens, lawful resident aliens of the United States, or any other persons who are *captured or arrested in the United States.*" So that section contains a disclaimer regarding an intention to expand detention powers for U.S. citizens, but does so only for the powers vested by that specific section. More important, the exclusion appears to extend *only* to U.S. citizens "captured or arrested *in the United States*"—meaning that the powers of indefinite detention vested by that section *apply to U.S. citizens captured anywhere abroad* (there is some grammatical vagueness on this point, but at the very least, there is a viable argument that the detention power in this section applies to U.S. citizens captured abroad).

But the next section, Section 1022, is a different story. That section specifically deals with a smaller category of people than the broad group covered by 1021: namely, anyone whom the President determines is "a member of, or part of, al-Qaeda or an associated force" and "participated in the course of planning or carrying out an attack or attempted attack against the United States or its coalition partners." For those persons, section (a) not only authorizes, but *requires* (absent a Presidential waiver), that they be held "in military custody pending disposition under the law of war." The section title is "Military Custody for Foreign Al Qaeda Terrorists," but the definition of who it covers does not exclude U.S. citizens or include any requirement of foreignness.

That section—1022—does *not* contain the broad disclaimer regarding U.S. citizens that 1021 contains. Instead, it simply says that *the requirement* of military detention does not apply to U.S. citizens, but it does not exclude U.S. citizens from the *authority, the option*, to hold them in military custody. Here is what it says:

> (b) Applicability to United States Citizens and Lawful Resident Aliens.—
>
> 1. United states citizens—The requirement to detain a person in military custody under this section does not extend to citizens of the United States.

The only provision from which U.S. citizens are exempted here is the *"requirement"* of military detention. For foreign nationals accused of being members of Al Qaeda, military detention is *mandatory*; for U.S. citizens, it is *optional*. This section does *not* exempt U.S citizens from the presidential power of military detention: only from the *requirement* of military detention.

The most important point on this issue is the same as underscored in the prior two points: the "compromise" reached by Congress includes language preserving the status quo. That's because the Obama administration already argues that the original 2001 AUMF authorizes them to act against U.S. citizens (obviously, if they believe they have the power to target U.S. citizens for assassination, then they believe they have the power to detain U.S. citizens as enemy combatants). The proof that this bill does not expressly exempt U.S. citizens or those captured on U.S. soil is that amendments offered by Sen. [Dianne] Feinstein providing expressly for those exemptions were rejected. The "compromise" was to preserve the status quo by including the provision that the bill is not intended to alter it with regard to American citizens, but that's because proponents of broad detention powers are confident that the status quo already permits such detention.

A Dangerous Bill

In sum, there is simply no question that this bill codifies indefinite detention without trial (Myth 1). There is no question that it significantly expands the statutory definitions of the War on Terror and those who can be targeted as part of it (Myth 2). The issue of application to U.S. citizens (Myth 3) is purposely muddled—that's why Feinstein's amendments were rejected—and there is consequently no doubt this bill can and will be used by the U.S. Government (under this President or a future one) to bolster its argument that it is empowered to indefinitely detain even U.S. citizens without a trial (*NYT* Editorial: "The legislation could also give future presidents the authority to throw American citizens into prison for life without charges or a trial"; Sen. Bernie Sanders: "This bill also contains misguided provisions that in the name of fighting terrorism essentially authorize the indefinite imprisonment of American citizens without charges").

Even if it were true that this bill changes nothing when compared to how the Executive Branch has been interpreting and exercising the powers of the old AUMF, there are serious dangers and harms from having Congress—with bipartisan sponsors, a Democratic Senate and a GOP [Republican] House—put its institutional, statutory weight behind powers previously claimed and seized by the President alone. That codification entrenches these powers. As the *New York Times* Editorial today put it: the bill contains "terrible new measures that will make indefinite detention and military trials *a permanent part of American law.*"

What's particularly ironic (and revealing) about all of this is that former White House counsel Greg Craig assured *The New Yorker's* Jane Mayer back in February 2009 that it's "*hard to imagine Barack Obama as the first President of the United States to introduce a preventive-detention law.*" Four months later, President Obama proposed exactly such a law—one that *The New York Times* described as "a departure from the way this country sees itself, as a place where people in the grip of the government either face criminal charges or walk free"—and now he will sign such a scheme into law.

| *"Although removal proceedings are administrative-civil in nature, over the course of time they have taken on many of the trappings of a criminal proceeding."*

Illegal Aliens Are Granted Excessive Due Process Rights

W.D. Reasoner

In the following viewpoint, W.D. Reasoner argues that although due process rights for illegal immigrants can be set by Congress, over time the due process accorded illegal aliens has expanded in an unsustainable fashion. Reasoner claims that there are a large number of alien fugitives—those who have fled from court proceedings—too many of whom are set free to wait for a judicial hearing or granted voluntary return, rather than being subject to expedited removal. W.D. Reasoner, which is a pseudonym, is a retired government employee with experience in immigration administration, law enforcement, and national security matters.

As you read, consider the following questions:

1. According to the author, up to how many alien fugitives are at large in the United States?

W.D. Reasoner, "Deportation Basics: How Immigration Enforcement Works (or Doesn't) in Real Life," *Backgrounder*, July 2011, pp. 2–4, 8–10, 12. Copyright © 2011 by Center For Immigration Studies. All rights reserved. Reproduced by permission.

2. According to Reasoner, what are two reasons an illegal alien would opt for voluntary return?
3. What percentage of aliens apprehended for immigration violations in fiscal year 2010 were permitted to voluntarily return to their home country, according to the author?

The Supreme Court has said that, where expulsion proceedings are concerned, due process for aliens in the United States is whatever Congress chooses it to be—subject to certain constraints imposed by the Constitution, and as ultimately interpreted by the courts themselves, that is.

A Hierarchy of Due Process

Over time, by means of law, regulation, and binding precedent decisions, a kind of hierarchy of due process rights has evolved for aliens who are placed into removal proceedings:

- Aliens who have entered and remain in the United States illegally are, understandably, accorded the least amount of due process.

- Nonimmigrant aliens, who may have originally entered legally, but later overstayed or otherwise violated the conditions of their admission, have somewhat more due process.

- Lawful resident aliens who are alleged to have committed some act rendering them removable (by commission of a crime, for example) are entitled to the most due process under the law based on their status and "equities" in the United States. The term "equities" usually refers to close family members, especially U.S.-born children, but also refers to ties to the community, stable employment, and length of residence in the United States for purposes of seeking a cancellation of removal.

However, this hierarchy is not hard and fast, and a major factor that enters into how, and what kind of, removal proceedings are commenced revolves around the legal charges filed against the alien: Certain removal charges carry with them the requirement, or at least the opportunity on the part of the government, to initiate certain kinds of proceedings that take place outside the parameters of the immigration court. What is more, it is at the discretion of the government to decide whether to lodge formal charges against an alien, to decide what charges to lodge, and such decisions are inevitably influenced by cost and economy. For example, the government may choose to permit a criminal alien to request "voluntary departure" in lieu of holding him in detention for an extended period of time while a removal hearing is conducted by an immigration judge.

Although removal proceedings are administrative-civil in nature, over the course of time they have taken on many of the trappings of a criminal proceeding—at least, those removal proceedings that are conducted by immigration judges have—albeit with differing standards for introduction of evidence and adjudication of removability (among other differences, the "beyond a reasonable doubt" standard doesn't apply). Such trappings include, among other things:

- issuance of warrants of arrest,
- provision of an advice of rights to aliens taken into custody,
- setting of a bond or other form of pre-hearing conditional release, and
- the right to counsel (at no expense to the government).

As mentioned, many removal proceedings take place in front of an immigration judge, who is responsible for conducting an impartial hearing, listening to testimony, accepting evidence, reviewing and ruling on legal motions and briefs from both sides, and arriving ultimately at a decision as to whether the alien should be removed from the United States. Just as with other "judicial" proceedings, such hearings can take a substantial amount of time (and money), may involve a number of continuances and adjournments, and, if the alien flees, result in an unenforceable order of removal until such time as he can be found and taken back into custody.

The Large Volume of Alien Fugitives

Aliens who flee from proceedings are traditionally called "absconders" or, more recently, "alien fugitives." The number of such individuals is high—perhaps as many as 5 percent of *the total number of aliens illegally in the United States*, according to past estimates. Various sources put the number of aliens illegally in the United States between 10 and 12 million, meaning that there may be up to 500,000–600,000 alien fugitives at large, a significant number of whom are removable based on criminal convictions. Note that this percentage calculation is based on the number of fugitives compared with all aliens in the United States—*not* just those who were put into proceedings and fled. If couched solely in the context of the percentage of aliens who are put into proceedings and abscond, the percentage would be more relevant—and much, much higher—perhaps as high as 59 percent of all aliens arrested and then conditionally released to await their hearings. That may be why the government has often chosen not to put it into that context; it becomes a stark reminder of the failure of the present system, and the softer number of 5 percent masks the level of dysfunction.

Considered logically, the large volume of alien fugitives should not be a surprise. If an alien absconds and is later captured, what is the worst he can expect? To be removed—the same thing that will happen if he sticks around. So on a cost-basis analysis from the alien's perspective, absconding makes sense: If you are in proceedings, and have few equities and no reasonable basis to believe you will be permitted to stay, why not choose to treat the bond money you've posted more as a fine and accept its loss—the cost of having been caught—and flee, hoping to stay under the radar for as long as possible. Who knows? With luck, maybe you can even remain undetected until there is a new amnesty program under which you might qualify to stay in the United States.

A Perpetual Logjam of Cases

The large number of absconders begs the question: Why does the government accept this state of affairs, being as it is *de facto* evidence of a system's fundamental inadequacies? Why not, for instance, keep more aliens in detention? There are a number of answers to these questions, which run the gamut from legal, procedural, and fiscal realities on one hand, to policy, philosophy, and politics on the other hand.

But one probable reason for the high absconder rate, though it remains publicly unacknowledged, is the length of time it takes for a removal proceeding to begin for aliens falling into the "non-detained docket." The perpetual logjam of cases within the immigration courts has become a cause of scrutiny by various organizations and legal groups that favor looser rules, including the American Bar Association (ABA) and the Migration Policy Institute (MPI). In its report, the ABA's Commission on Immigration found that 231 immigration judges nationwide hear more than 280,000 proceedings each year—an average of 1,243 per judge. Because detained cases constitute the priority docket for immigration judges, court backlogs for non-detained cases are often well over a year long before the hearing even commences. Many aliens, following the seasonal flow of jobs, or out of indifference, or with well-thought-out intent, choose to get on with their lives and disappear.

Perhaps not surprisingly, given their philosophical focus as migrant and defense advocacy groups, neither the ABA nor MPI advocate more streamlined or additional use of non-judicial forms of due process. Instead, they suggest a substantial increase in the number of judges and support staff; additional opportunities for the use of alien defense lawyers ("attorneys for the respondent" in the parlance of immigration removal proceedings); more, and increased grants of, types of relief from removal;

expansion of the appellate rights of aliens in removal proceedings; and additional use of "prosecutorial discretion" in deciding whom to arrest versus whom to ignore among the illegal alien population of the United States.

ICE [Immigration and Customs Enforcement] Director John Morton in fact issued a policy memorandum on March 2, 2011—virtually at the same time that the MPI issued its report and within weeks after the ABA issued its report—that encourages the exercise of prosecutorial discretion by field officers in their daily enforcement activities, citing, among other documents, a memorandum from prior Immigration and Naturalization Service (INS) Commissioner Doris Meissner, who is now a Senior Fellow with MPI and co-author of its report.

The Problem with Prosecutorial Discretion

Although transparently simple on its face, the difficulty with the exercise of prosecutorial discretion, from the perspective of field officers, is this: Should they release an individual who appears to meet the guidelines, but later commits a heinous act, there is no assurance that they will not be second-guessed as to whether the alien should have been released. Given the treacherous nature of immigration politics, and the fact that they are not immune to civil tort suits from survivor victims or family members subsequent to such an act committed by a released alien, this fear justifiably looms large in the minds of field officers and agents, who know full well that they are at risk on two fronts: from lawsuits and from "hindsight is 20-20" perspective of their own agency and department.

ICE has also chosen another tack in exercising prosecutorial discretion to deal with the burgeoning court backlogs. In recent months, media reports from various cities throughout the country have reported government trial attorneys filing hundreds of motions before immigration judges for case dismissals, based on loose criteria such as the alien having "no serious criminal history." It seems a rather curious solution to the problem, given the thousands of productive hours that must have already been invested by officers and agents in apprehending and processing the aliens whose cases were dismissed, insofar as it reflects a kind of organizational binge-and-purge mindset at work. What is more, there has been no public indicator that prior to moving for dismissal, any significant effort was invested by the government in determining whether the aliens had already absconded while waiting for their hearing to commence. This approach leads to three questions: (1) Why should persons who may have fled accrue the benefit of a dismissal? It seems fundamentally unfair. (2) Why should illegal aliens respect the established immigration removal hearing process when it becomes clear through wholesale dismissals that the government itself does not? (3) What valid strategic goal or public purpose is being served through these dismissals? The aliens whose cases have been dismissed don't accrue any benefit or right to remain legally. To the contrary, they have not-so-subtly been encouraged to drift back into the sub-rosa [under-the-radar] community and economy of illegals living and working in the United States. . . .

The Option to Voluntarily Depart

The Immigration and Nationality Act (INA) provides for several types of due process to be accorded to an alien, depending on the facts and circumstances surrounding his entry into, and stay in, the United States—e.g., whether the initial entry was legal or not, whether he has been convicted of a crime, the type of crime committed, etc. . . .

Voluntary Return [VR] may be granted by federal officers in lieu of presenting an alien to an immigration judge for a removal hearing. Technically, VR constitutes a request by an alien to be permitted to return to his country of citizenship or nativity on a voluntary basis. Aliens who are removable as aggravated felons, or under the national security-terrorism grounds laid out in the INA, are not eligible for VR. The statute provides that an alien must pay his own fare to be eligible for VR, but the reality is that almost no alien reimburses the government the funds for his repatriation.

In the course of a hearing, a judge may also grant an alien the opportunity to voluntarily depart in lieu of a formal order of removal. If, however, the request for VR is made by the alien (or his counsel) at the conclusion of the hearing, then in addition to the requirements mentioned above, he must show physical presence in the United States for at least a year prior to issuance of the NTA [Note to Appear in Removal Proceedings], prove good moral character for the past five years, and not have been convicted of criminal offenses evincing moral turpitude.

It needs to be understood that voluntary removal isn't particularly "voluntary," at least as a layman might conceive of it. This is because in most instances, the alien will be held in detention pending his departure; and the departure, when it occurs, will be under safeguards—that is to say, he will be escorted by armed, uniformed ICE officers to ensure that he in fact leaves the United States.

The Problem with Voluntary Return

Why, then, would an alien opt for such an arrangement? The first has to do with a desire on the part of the alien not to spend inordinate amounts of time in detention when he knows he has no basis to remain. The second reason has to do with an understanding that, by departing voluntarily instead of being formally removed, he escapes the possibility of being criminally charged with a federal felony for reentry after removal, should he choose to return illegally in the future, and again get caught—aliens are often highly aware of the nuances and complexities of immigration law, given its impact on their lives.

Given the reduced penalties an alien incurs should he illegally reenter, why would federal officers opt to grant Voluntary Removal to an alien instead of pursuing a formal order of removal? Sheer volume. Granting voluntary departure aids the government in getting aliens out of the country quickly and economically. Mexican nationals are often recipients of VR.

The problem with VR is that it is subject to overuse or misuse—including in cases where prudence (or, occasionally, even the law) dictate that it should not be granted. For instance, on October 6, 2010, the *Los Angeles Times* reported that the administration had removed a record 392,862 aliens—nearly half of whom were criminals—in FY [fiscal year] 2009. Director Morton was quoted as saying, "ICE is committed to tough law enforcement."

But by December 5, the *Washington Post* was reporting that to achieve those numbers, ICE officials had "quietly directed immigration officers to bypass backlogged immigration courts and time-consuming deportation hearings whenever possible, internal e-mails and interviews show. Instead, officials told immigration officers to encourage eligible foreign nationals to accept a quick pass to their countries without a negative mark on their immigration record, ICE employees said. The option, known as voluntary return, may have allowed hundreds of immigrants— who typically would have gone before an immigration judge to contest deportation for offenses such as drunken driving, domestic violence, and misdemeanor assault—to leave the country . . ." without formally being ordered removed. Morton was obliged to respond publicly in order to deny that the agency had "cooked the books" to meet its own goals. . . .

Expedited Removal Proceedings

In 1996 Congress, recognizing the need for reform in the due process being provided to illegal alien border crossers—and in an attempt to unburden immigration courts of case backlogs existing even then—passed the Illegal Immigration Reform and Immigrant Responsibility Act (IIRIRA), which was quickly signed into law by the President. IIRIRA amended the INA to establish a non-judicial expedited removal provision permitting the Attorney General to designate, by promulgation in the

Federal Register, those classes of aliens to whom this type of proceeding would apply provided, at minimum, that they:

- are applicants for admission to the United States; or
- have entered the United States without admission or parole, and have been continuously physically present in the United States for less than two years (in which case they are to be treated as applicants for admission);
- are inadmissible under certain statutory grounds primarily due to failure to comply with visa or other entry document requirements, and/or fraud or misrepresentation;
- make no claim to lawful resident alien status; and
- do not seek asylum or express a fear of persecution.

The law and regulations provide that immigration inspectors or examining immigration officers (which include the apprehending officers or agents of the Border Patrol, ICE or other DHS [Department of Homeland Security] agencies) may issue an order of removal against an alien who falls within the parameters of this section. However, before the order becomes final, it must be reviewed and approved by a supervisory officer. Further, if an alien is charged in expedited removal proceedings, no other removal charges may be lodged. Most aliens removed under this provision of law are barred from reentry for five years, although for certain categories of aliens, the bar is for life.

Unfortunately, in the 15 years since this provision was enacted into law, the federal government has been extraordinarily cautious in expanding it by regulation to its fullest potential reach. At the present time, it is applied only to applicants for admission at ports of entry, or to aliens encountered within 100 miles of the land or maritime borders who have entered the United States without inspection *less than 14 days* before the time they are encountered. In other words, it is a tool of some utility for border officers, but of little or no use to those federal officers charged with immigration enforcement in the interior of the United States where the lion's share of the population of 10 to 12 million aliens live. . . .

There are two fundamental reasons for restricting the unbridled use of voluntary return. First, no alien convicted of a crime should be granted the privilege of voluntary return. Doing so undermines the stated DHS and ICE priorities of focusing immigration enforcement efforts on alien criminals. ICE Director Morton should issue a policy directive requiring the use of formal proceedings against alien criminals so that orders of removal, with the attendant criminal sanctions for reentry after removal, are obtained. Second, VR encourages recidivists to illegally return to the United States with little or no credible fear of consequences because it eliminates the possibility of a criminal prosecution for reentry after removal. Consider: in FY 2010, DHS officers apprehended a total of 516,992 aliens for immigration violations. Of these, 476,405—fully 92 percent—were permitted to voluntarily return to their home country in lieu of proceedings. And yet, most of these aliens (463,382—89.6 percent of the total apprehensions) were taken into custody by the Border Patrol agents in proximity to America's physical frontiers and most could have been formally removed by use of expedited removal.

> *"The rot at the core of many immigration proceedings . . . deprives the public of confidence that the hundreds of thousands of people being kicked out are genuinely deportable."*

Lawless Courts

Jacqueline Stevens

In the following viewpoint, Jacqueline Stevens argues that there is rampant disregard for the due process rights of individuals within the immigration court system. Stevens claims that individuals, including some US citizens, are often hastily deported. She contends that the lack of transparency and the culture of protecting misconduct must change, and she suggests a change in leadership of the Executive Office of Immigration Review (EOIR). Stevens is a professor in the Political Science Department at Northwestern University and the author of States Without Nations: Citizenship for Mortals.

As you read, consider the following questions:

1. According to Stevens, what federal agency is responsible for running immigration hearings?
2. How many cases were initiated in the immigration courts in 2009, according to the author?

3. What percentage of people in immigration jails lack attorneys, according to Stevens?

One day in April, J. Dan Pelletier, a government adjudicator, faces a video camera in an Atlanta immigration court. At the same moment, in a Stewart Detention Center mini-court in the Georgia hinterland, two dozen men in orange and blue jumpsuits seated behind a low rail are watching Pelletier on a monitor wheeled in front of a vacant dais. Pelletier addresses the men brusquely: "I have been told each of you has admitted the allegations and conceded removability back to your home country. Is there anybody in this group that does not want an order of removal to their home country?"

Giving the men no time for comprehension or to summon the courage to reply, Pelletier pushes on, ignoring the rule requiring him to ascertain whether each individual is abandoning a claim to remain in the United States. The interpreter, also in Atlanta, repeats in Spanish, "Nobody said anything. Does each one accept this? Please respond in the affirmative." The men sit there, mute, befuddled, watching the cranky old man like they might watch any other bad TV. The Department of Homeland Security (DHS) prosecutor sits quietly in front of the rail.

Pelletier says, "I'm asking each of you to please respond orally." A few say yes or *sí* in a tone bespeaking a desire to end their confinement and stop the badgering. Many say nothing. No one has a lawyer.

Pelletier, who has the job title "immigration judge" but is employed by the Justice Department and not the judiciary, says, "If you object, say something. If you remain silent I will issue the order in each case."

Immigration court rules state, "It would offend due process if the immigration judge obtains from the group a 'mass silent waiver of the right of appeal.'" Nonetheless, Pelletier says, "I will take their silence as a waiver of their right to appeal, and I will issue an order," deporting the men en masse. Guards usher them to the hall, but four men are agitated and lag behind. "Hey," says one, "I thought we were going to talk to the judge!" Too late, a guard says, and orders them into the hall. One obeys. The DHS prosecutor notices the commotion, and at my prompting, she requests that Pelletier reopen the cases of the three still there.

Victor, 24, has been in the United States lawfully since arriving from Guatemala when he was 3. (Immigration and Customs Enforcement, or ICE, targeted him because of a seven-month misdemeanor marijuana conviction.) The DHS attorney looks through his file and tells Pelletier that Victor's mother probably included him as a dependent on her asylum application. Pelletier says he is "not comfortable" issuing an order against him, adding, "You may have an unadjusted status," meaning that Victor can apply for legal residency and be free pending a final decision.

This is Victor's big break, his reward for fighting for a hearing. Victor, however, confused by Pelletier's expression of discomfort and irritated demeanor, to say nothing of the legal gobbledegook, says, "I'll take the removal because my daughter needs my help, and I cannot do it behind bars." Suddenly Victor is heading to Guatemala, a country he hasn't seen since infancy.

Pelletier and his colleagues are able to run roughshod over the rights of US residents because the agency that runs immigration hearings, the pompous and obscurely titled Executive Office of Immigration Review (EOIR), headquartered in Falls Church, Virginia, is a paranoid bureaucratic backwater that shields immigration judges from accountability. As long as adjudicators process a high volume of cases, the agency will ignore and even cover up serious misconduct, including deportations of US citizens or people who have other avenues of relief. One immigration judge told me, "I'm afraid there's a premium on quotas and productivity, and not the truth."

The vast number of cases handled by Pelletier and William Cassidy, another Atlanta adjudicator, has made them into agency superstars. In 2008, 83 percent of the respondents held in Georgia's Stewart Detention Center were ordered deported, virtually all by Cassidy and Pelletier, compared with 72 percent nationwide. Glenn Fogle, an Atlanta immigration attorney, says of the ICE and EOIR operation at Stewart, "They're basically a deportation machine, trying to use the discretion of the judge, who's not following the law but making his own law."

Fogle expresses frustration that Pelletier, Cassidy and a third Atlanta adjudicator, Grace Sease, are all former DHS attorneys. "They're your archenemies for fifteen years and now they're the judge," he says. A new hire at the Stewart court also comes from ICE.

The disregard for due process in Georgia, which has the country's third-largest docket and respondents from across the country, is a national catastrophe—although the effects are personal to Logan Guzman, a 3-year-old who for more than a year has missed the affection of his father, Pedro, because Cassidy is resisting a recommendation from the Board of Immigration Appeals to grant Pedro bond based on his close ties to US citizens. (Cassidy turned this around, ruling that these close ties would make Pedro a flight risk and held him even though Guzman had a slam-dunk case on the merits.) Fogle, Guzman's attorney, says, "That's the logic of someone who wants to keep somebody in jail no matter what, to make them give up on their case and leave. That's this whole system, not just [Cassidy]. It's a strategy used by the DHS. You don't give someone a bond or give them a high bond, and they'll give up on their case and just leave."

Some adjudicators, relying on "stipulated removal orders," are deporting people without even seeing them. According to Rachel Rosenbloom, a professor at Northeastern Law School, an immigration judge who insists on "thoroughly questioning" people who sign these orders "regularly encounters US citizens." Rosenbloom adds, "There are many judges who don't question people, and it's very likely there's going to be US citizens among those people as well, and they're not being [identified]." (The

EOIR statistics on the citizenship of respondents in immigration courts come from DHS filings, not the adjudicator decisions. As a result, even though thousands of citizens have been in deportation proceedings, the official EOIR number is zero.)

The country's 238 adjudicators in fifty-nine immigration courts rule on everything from asylum applications to whether a marijuana conviction warrants deportation. Many, especially the good ones, are burned out from their share of the massive annual caseload: 390,000 cases were initiated across the country in 2009. The laws, regulations and infrastructure are inadequate to the high stakes of prolonged incarceration or banishment. Dana Marks, leader of the immigration judge union—which has been pushing Congress for more personnel and logistical support, and independence from the Justice Department—says, "We're doing death penalty cases in traffic court settings." Marks's union presidency exempts her from the agency's ban on its employees' speaking to the media.

The rot at the core of many immigration proceedings, especially in detention centers, where 50 percent of all hearings were held in 2009, up from 30 percent in 2005, deprives the public of confidence that the hundreds of thousands of people being kicked out are genuinely deportable. The Boston College Post-Deportation and Human Rights Project receives inquiries from people worldwide and has identified dozens of US residents unlawfully shipped back to their countries of origin. The group is joining other advocates in pressing for legal changes to allow former US residents to reopen their cases from abroad.

The Post-Deportation Project, formerly known as Ruby Slippers, has an office in Zacualpa, Guatemala, and is establishing points of contact in the Azores and Ecuador for research and legal assistance. Referring to the thousands of unlawful deportations, co-director Daniel Kanstroom, a Boston College law professor, says, "We're only limited by the number of lawyers we can hire."

The underlying problems go back to the Clinton administration's support of the bad 1996 immigration law and bad ad-

The Lack of Resources in Immigration Courts

There is general agreement that the immigration courts need substantially more resources in order to do their inherently difficult job. Current resources provide too few immigration judges (IJs) and thus impose case processing demands on them that greatly exceed demands on other adjudicators whose decisions can have momentous impact. IJs in 2009 averaged 1,251 completed proceedings per judge, with considerable variation among the courts—from 506 per judge in one court to 3,504 in another. By contrast, federal district judges in 2009 terminated on average 528 civil cases and criminal defendants per judgeship, and few argue that federal district judges are underworked. IJs have an especially difficult job because of their working conditions, the kind of evidence before them, and because their decisions, some literally involving life or death, are largely dichotomous—removal or not rather than, for example, the range of criminal sentences a judge could impose—and their decisions are final, as opposed, for example, to state criminal sentences that a parole board can reconsider.

Russell R. Wheeler, Congressional Testimony, June 17, 2010.

judicators. In 1999 John Zastrow, employed as an adjudicator since 1983, deported Johann Francis, a US citizen, from the Eloy Detention Center in Arizona to Jamaica. It took Francis ten years to return. (Following a 1998 teenage brawl, Francis, then 19, completed a six-month sentence at an Oregon boot camp. The day of his release, without warning, he was picked up by immigration agents and shipped to Eloy.)

According to Francis's file, an agent at Eloy filled out a "Request for a Prompt Removal," but Francis never saw or signed it. Nonetheless, on April 7, 1999, without a hearing, Zastrow ordered Francis deported. Two months later, still in Eloy and unaware of Zastrow's ruling, Francis followed the instructions of a deportation officer and hand-wrote a request to be deported so he could leave confinement. "I guess it was just a CYA [cover your ass] thing," he now says of this document. "How can this happen in America?"

In late June 1999 Francis, "the guy who runs for school president," as he puts it, was sleeping on the streets in Kingston; he later moved to a rural area, where he survived on coconuts. "You drink two and you'll be full," he explains, adding that he became very sick from malnourishment.

He was stuck there even after he found his mother two years later. "I was able to prove who my mother was," he says, but since Jamaica filed birth certificates by number, not name, "I couldn't prove who *I* was." After Jamaica digitized its birth certificate registry, Francis was able to apply for a passport and return home in late 2009. He is now advising two other men in Jamaica, one deported last year, struggling to document their own US citizenship. Zastrow's last year on the job was 2000, but the federal courts are still overturning his orders for the few lucky enough to return for a hearing. And the decades-old pattern of wrongful deportations is continuing under the Obama administration.

Among those stuck in immigration jails today are people with no criminal history and, crucially, no lawyers to demand bond hearings. People who should be free may languish for months. When I met Clifford Bryan in Stewart, he was crying and contemplating suicide, largely because the adjudicators refused to grant a bond hearing and he feared being stuck there forever. "I filled out the paper [requesting a bond hearing] and sent it two times. They didn't send it back to me," he said. He was held for almost four months in Georgia before Cassidy finally set a $1,500 bond, the lowest amount possible, and Bryan was free to return to his wife in Michigan. Meanwhile, taxpayers had paid about $8,000 to the Corrections Corporation of America for his incarceration. In October the DHS issued welcome new rules resulting in ICE freeing hundreds nationwide, but many more who meet the criteria for release remain locked up, including Pedro Guzman.

The public's ignorance of the idiocies endemic to the EOIR's business as usual and the calamities these entail is no accident. The agency deliberately withholds basic information from the media and researchers, and its top officials routinely decline requests for interviews, as acting director Thomas Snow and others did twice for this article. (Snow is "acting," so he won't lose his civil-service job in the EOIR.)

According to David Burnham, a former *New York Times* reporter and co-director of the Transactional Records Access Clearinghouse, the staff in the EOIR public affairs office have a "bizarre conception of their role. We ask simple administrative questions and they say, Oh, you have to submit a FOIA request." Lauren Alder Reid, the agency's public affairs legal counsel, sent numerous e-mails along these lines to me but, along with top agency officials, is not responding to document requests from the agency's FOIA office as required by law.

The EOIR obscures its operations as well by admonishing immigration judges not to speak with the media, in contrast with other adjudicative agencies and the judiciary. When alerted to this, Charles Geyh, a law professor at the University of Indiana and a reporter for the American Bar Association's *Model Code of Judicial Conduct*, sounded taken aback. With the exception of prohibiting judges from commenting on pending cases, "it's not just that the rules say that you can do it, but they actively encourage it. Banning it makes the process seem less transparent and doesn't promote the confidence in the courts we're trying to encourage. Not conveying to the public the work they do and why they do it and how they do it is nonsense."

Even the court hearings are hidden from public scrutiny, especially those in detention centers, despite a regulation requiring otherwise. In August Dan Kowalski, an immigration attorney in Austin, Texas, and editor of *Bender's Immigration Bulletin*, sent the EOIR an e-mail asking whether the public would be allowed to attend hearings at a new court in the Pearsall, Texas, detention center. Kowalski explained his concern to me: "Sunlight is the best disinfectant. If there's nobody watching, it's easier for the prosecutors and immigration judges to take shortcuts or be dismissive or even abusive with the respondents." The EOIR's public affairs officer, Elaine Komis, replied to Kowalski's query by telling him to "contact GEO," a private security firm under contract to the DHS.

GEO's track record is bleak, according to Sandy Restrepo, an ACLU policy intern in Washington State. "Community members and law students...are getting hassled or turned away by security when they come in to watch the immigration hearings" at the Tacoma Detention Center run by GEO, Restrepo wrote in her July message to an immigration advocate listserv. Restrepo told me that since a 2008 Seattle University report documenting GEO's mistreatment of people in its custody, there have been "constant problems" with court access. She blames the EOIR as well as GEO. "The court administrator doesn't want a similar type of report to come out" about the Tacoma immigration courts, Restrepo believes.

Irina Kalinka, a Bard College student, decided that for her spring research project she would attend hearings at a nearby immigration court housed in the Downstate Prison in Fishkill, New York. The Fishkill EOIR office said she should call the prison for "security clearance." After being transferred to different prison personnel and calling several times, she was told by a prison official to fax a letter to the "Central Office." She asked where that was. "After a long silence," Kalinka wrote in an e-mail, "he just hung up." She left messages, but no one called her back. "The process of trying to find access is not just confusing," she wrote, "but I would go so far as to say actively discouraging." Kowalski suggests relocating the courts to a "different part of the building that doesn't need so much security, or give up on the notion of having them in the detention center altogether."

An employee of the immigration court in the agency's head-quarters in Falls Church, Virginia, concerned I might be with the media, would not allow me to attend a hearing even after I had passed security; she was overruled by a superior, who said this was a "mistake." Despite a regulation stipulating that hearings are open to the public, another official disclosed a policy requiring court personnel to ascertain if an observer is with the media before entrance is allowed.

On my entering the hearing, immigration judge Roxanne Hladylowycz announced to the respondent, her attorney and the DHS attorney that an observer had entered her courtroom and indicated that she was not asking their permission for the observer to remain. Immigration courts are open to the public, she explained to a group in Memphis, who appeared on a huge, gorgeous flat-screen worthy of the Super Bowl. "She has a right to be here."

And then I observed a fascinating and scrupulously well-run hearing in which Hladylowycz figured out that the government's claim of fraud was based on confusion arising from the fact that the respondent, Alina, and her sister, despite both taking on their husbands' last names, had married men with the same last name. Alina's hearing took about an hour, sixty minutes longer than those for people in mass removal hearings.

Complaints about immigration judges fall under the jurisdiction of the Office of Professional Responsibility (OPR), and people may file there directly, but the EOIR instructs immigration court stakeholders to lodge complaints with the EOIR itself. Instead of passing complaints on to the OPR, as the website promises, the EOIR top brass, to protect their cronies and avoid outside scrutiny, sweeps complaints under the rug. From September

2009 to August 2010, none of the OPR investigations originated with misconduct complaints filed with the EOIR. All but one occurred when federal courts overruled immigration judge decisions, per OPR policy. Since more than 84 percent of people in immigration jails lack attorneys and may submit complaints to the EOIR but will not file appeals in federal court, the OPR will never learn of most misconduct.

The EOIR batted away my recent complaint documenting extensive misconduct over the past eighteen months by Cassidy, who has worked in EOIR headquarters, and the Atlanta court administrator, Cynthia Long, including criminal and civil lawbreaking. The information should have been passed on to the OPR and the Office of the Inspector General, but according to EOIR attorney Mary Beth Keller, it stayed in-house at the EOIR.

Protecting misconduct is old news at the EOIR, which has been receiving complaints about Cassidy for years, including in the late 1990s from David Farshy, an attorney who attracted Cassidy's ire for protesting his due process violations. In one case, Cassidy left a message on Farshy's answering machine revealing an unlawful private conversation with the government's attorney and stating that he had decided Farshy's client's case before the hearing. Rather than fire Cassidy for these flagrant violations, the agency hired the government attorney with whom he'd had the conversation—Sease, now an Atlanta adjudicator who attracts her own misconduct complaints.

The experience of Adolfo Equite-Sequen, who lived in Los Angeles for twenty years and is eligible to apply for a green card, is another chilling example of the effects of moving DHS prosecutors from behind the table to behind the judge's bench. In September 2009, Equite was arrested for public drunkenness and, because of ethnic profiling, sent to ICE custody. A few days later he was shipped to Eloy based on an unauthenticated fingerprint match with the record of someone whose first name is Martin and who was ordered deported in 2004. ICE claimed no records existed for Equite.

Linda Spencer-Walters was a DHS attorney in 2008. In February 2010, she was Equite's adjudicator. Relying solely on the evidence from her old office, she discredited all of Equite's statements, denied bond and would not reopen his case even after a nonprofit attorney proved the DHS possessed Equite's bona fide immigration file.

Equite's pending appeal points out that Spencer-Walters ignored blatant inconsistencies in the ICE arrest report and admitted into evidence an unauthenticated fingerprint associated with a signature that did not match that of Equite, now in Guatemala.

Sarah Owings, EOIR liaison for the Atlanta chapter of the American Immigration Lawyers Association last year, said of similar events she has observed in immigration hearings, "Things are happening so quickly. They're trusting ICE has done their job and done the paperwork. They're not acting as adjudicators when they only get one side of the story and it may not be correct." Dana Marks sums up the problem: "As long as we are housed in the culture of a law enforcement agency, it's going to be difficult to achieve judicial neutrality." But severing the EOIR from the Justice Department, and the union's other worthwhile objectives, could take years.

Starting today, Attorney General Eric Holder can appoint a new director for the EOIR, ideally someone who will run this law enforcement agency according to the rule of law. The Justice Department could also issue new regulations for the EOIR to achieve immigration reforms that may not be possible through Congress or the DHS, including one mandating the release of anyone who is not given a bond hearing within forty-eight hours of a request. President Obama, whose own citizenship has been called into question, might want to take advantage of it.

Periodical and Internet Sources Bibliography

The following articles have been selected to supplement the diverse views presented in this chapter.

Mark Engler	"Guantanamo Has Got to Go: Protesting Ten Years of Indefinite Detention," *Dissent*, January 12, 2012.
John Griffing	"Obama, the Hitman: Killing Due Process," *American Thinker*, October 5, 2011. www.american thinker.com.
Murat Kurnaz	"Notes from a Guantanamo Survivor," *New York Times*, January 7, 2012.
Michelle Malkin	"How Mexico Treats Illegal Aliens," *Human Events*, April 28, 2010.
Wendy McElroy	"Due Process in Jeopardy: The Supreme Court Takes Liberty Lightly," *The Freeman*, May 24, 2010.
Andrew Napolitano	"Can the President Kill You?," *Reason*, March 14, 2012.
New York Sun	"'A Due Process in War,'" October 2, 2011.
Tom Parker	"10 Years On, 10 Reasons Guantanamo Must Be Closed," *Human Rights Now* (blog), January 11, 2012. http://blog .amnestyusa.org.
Adam Serwer	"When the Government Can Kill You, Explained," *Mother Jones*, March 5, 2012.
Howard Slugh	"Exclusionary Rule Unwarranted for GPS Searches," *National Review*, January 31, 2012.
Joe Wolverton II	"Is Julian Assange Being Denied Due Process?," *New American*, April 13, 2012.

CHAPTER 4

Is the Right to Privacy in Jeopardy?

Chapter Preface

The right to privacy, although not explicitly mentioned in the US Constitution, has come to be recognized as a fundamental right of all Americans. In 1886, the US Supreme Court first referred to "the sanctity of a man's home and the privacies of life."[1] In the last few decades, the right to privacy has become more explicitly protected through decisions of the court, which have recognized not only a right to privacy in one's home and possessions but also a right to privacy in reproductive decisions and in sexual relations; i.e., privacy with respect to one's body.

In the court's 1965 defense of privacy within the marital relationship for the purposes of using contraception, it identified several sources of the right to privacy within the Bill of Rights. Justice William O. Douglas explained how the court came to the conclusion that a right to privacy is implicit in the Constitution:

> Specific guarantees in the Bill of Rights have penumbras, formed by emanations from those guarantees that help give them life and substance. Various guarantees create zones of privacy. The right of association contained in the penumbra of the First Amendment is one. . . . The Third Amendment, in its prohibition against the quartering of soldiers "in any house" in time of peace without the consent of the owner, is another facet of that privacy. The Fourth Amendment explicitly affirms the "right of the people to be secure in their persons, houses, papers, and effects, against unreasonable searches and seizures." The Fifth Amendment, in its Self-Incrimination Clause, enables the citizen to create a zone of privacy which government may not force him to surrender to his detriment. The Ninth Amendment provides: "The enumeration in the Constitution, of certain rights, shall not be construed to deny or disparage others retained by the people."[2]

Thus, the right to privacy is seen as implicitly endorsed within the penumbras, or peripheries, of several amendments in the Bill of Rights. Not without controversy, the court's reasoning in this case came to be used to support the right to privacy in obtaining an abortion and in engaging in sexual contact with members of the same sex.

Beyond the realm of the home, reproduction, and intimate association, the right to privacy also protects certain activities in public. In 1967, the court ruled that warrantless electronic surveillance in a public telephone booth violated the right to privacy, noting, "the Fourth Amendment protects people—not places."[3] However, in recent years domestic surveillance undertaken in the name of national security has come under fire for violating the right to privacy. Several organizations, including the American Civil Liberties Union (ACLU), have filed a lawsuit challenging the Foreign Intelligence Surveillance Act that expanded the National Security Agency's warrantless wiretapping program.

The right to privacy of information is another area of recent controversy. In 1977, the court upheld a state law that required computerized records of individuals who obtained certain drugs by medical prescription. Although the court recognized "the threat to privacy implicit in the accumulation of vast amounts of personal information in computerized data banks or other massive government files,"[4] it noted that as long as private information is protected to avoid unwarranted disclosure, such collection of information does not necessarily violate the right to privacy. The growth of the Internet has prompted legislative protections for privacy, such as the Children's Internet Protection Act (2003), and discussions about further legislation are ongoing.

The right to privacy is one of the most cherished yet controversial rights in America. On the one hand, few would deny that some expectation of privacy constitutes a basic civil liberty; on the other hand, the expansion of the right to privacy to areas such as abortion has been very controversial. Recently, the War on Terrorism and the burgeoning use of the Internet have created numerous controversies regarding privacy rights. Balancing interests of privacy with interests of security (in the case of terrorism) or with interests of liberty (in the case of the Internet) has created much new debate about this fundamental liberty.

Notes

1. *Boyd v. United Stats*, 116 U.S. 616 (1886).
2. *Griswold v. Connecticut*, 1965.
3. *Katz v. United States*, 1967.
4. *Whalen v. Roe*, 429 U.S. 589 (1997).

| *"It's encouraging that the justices are no longer arguing about whether to regulate virtual surveillance in public but instead about how best to protect privacy in light of new technologies."*

All Hail Samuel Alito, Privacy Champion Extraordinaire!

Jeffrey Rosen

In the following viewpoint, Jeffrey Rosen argues that the US Supreme Court's decision in United States v. Jones *(2012) was an important victory for the right to privacy. Rosen claims that the majority opinion was correct to recognize that any physical intrusions on private property require a warrant. Furthermore, he claims that the reasoning expressed in concurring opinions bodes well for the outcome of future privacy cases regarding new surveillance technology. Rosen is a professor of law at George Washington University and the legal affairs editor of the* New Republic.

As you read, consider the following questions:

1. According to Rosen, which US Supreme Court justice authored the majority opinion in *United States v. Jones*?

2. Which Supreme Court justice does the author suggest is the top advocate for privacy?

3. What is the title of the legislation that Rosen endorses passing?

Yesterday the Supreme Court handed down the most important privacy case of the Roberts era, *US. v. Jones.* The unanimous decision is an occasion for dancing in the chat rooms. In holding that the government needs a warrant before attaching a GPS device to a suspect's car to track his movements 24/7 for a month, all the justices rejected the Obama administration's extreme and unnecessary position that we have no expectations of privacy when it comes to the virtual surveillance of our movements in public places. Although the majority decision is narrow and many hard cases involving virtual surveillance lie ahead, all of the justices acknowledged that round the clock surveillance is far more invasive than tracking someone's movements for a day. Now it's up to Congress to fill in the legal gaps for GPS tracking and for the Court to build on this landmark decision in future cases.

Writing for five of his colleagues, Justice Antonin Scalia's majority opinion focused on the fact that the police had committed a physical trespass when they put a GPS device on the bottom of a suspect's car without a valid warrant. "The government physically occupied private property for the purpose of obtaining information," Scalia wrote, explaining that such a physical intrusion doubtlessly qualifies as a "search."

Scalia's decision is welcome because it insists that even the smallest physical intrusions on private property require a warrant. But with his focus on physical trespass, Scalia does little to resolve the virtual surveillance questions that are on the horizon. As Justice Samuel Alito pointed out in his insightful concurrence—joined by Justices Ruth Bader Ginsburg, Stephen Breyer, and Elena Kagan—according to Scalia's reasoning the

New Devices and Privacy

Recent years have seen the emergence of many new devices that permit the monitoring of a person's movements. In some locales, closed-circuit television video monitoring is becoming ubiquitous. On toll roads, automatic toll collection systems create a precise record of the movements of motorists who choose to make use of that convenience. Many motorists purchase cars that are equipped with devices that permit a central station to ascertain the car's location at any time so that roadside assistance may be provided if needed and the car may be found if it is stolen.

Perhaps most significant, cell phones and other wireless devices now permit wireless carriers to track and record the location of users—and as of June 2011, it has been reported, there were more than 322 million wireless devices in use in the United States. For older phones, the accuracy of the location information depends on the density of the tower network, but new "smart phones," which are equipped with a GPS device, permit more precise tracking. For example, when a user activates the GPS on such a phone, a provider is able to monitor the phone's location and speed of movement and can then report back real-time traffic conditions after combining ("crowdsourcing") the speed of all such phones on any particular road. Similarly, phone-location-tracking services are offered as "social" tools, allowing consumers to find (or to avoid) others who enroll in these services. The availability and use of these and other new devices will continue to shape the average person's expectations about the privacy of his or her daily movements.

Samuel Alito, United States v. Jones,
January 23, 2012.

government would need a warrant to put a GPS device under a suspect's car but not to activate a GPS tracking system *already* embedded in the car. And, as Alito also noted, smartphones allow Apple (or the police) to track a user's movements 24/7 without any sort of physical trespass.

With his concurring opinion, Alito has cemented his reputation as the Supreme Court's top privacy cop—one of the justices most sensitive to the impact of new technologies on expectations of privacy. As a Princeton student in 1971, Alito chaired a student conference on surveillance technologies, which concluded, "We sense a great threat to privacy in modern America." In the *Jones* case, Alito proposed a welcome framework for meeting those threats, distinguishing between short-term monitoring and the longer-term GPS monitoring that impinges on our actual expectations of privacy. Refusing to identify the precise point between a day and a month when the surveillance becomes unconstitutional, Alito said that when the police are unsure, they can always get a warrant.

Justice Sonia Sotomayor, in a separate concurrence, indicated that she might in the future go further still. She asks if we should reconsider what's known as the "third party doctrine," which suggests that if I surrender my search terms to Google or my geolocation information to Apple, I have to assume the risk that Google and Apple will turn over that information to the government. Now that most of our private papers are stored not in locked desk drawers but on distributed servers in the digital cloud owned by Google and Yahoo, the Court does indeed need to revisit the third party doctrine if citizens are to have as much privacy in the twenty-first century as they did in the eighteenth. Given Sotomayor's willingness to go beyond Scalia in translating the Constitution in light of new technologies, it's surprising that she provided a fifth vote for his narrow opinion, rather than joining Alito and her liberal colleagues in making clear that the Constitution imposes limits on even long-term surveillance that *doesn't* involve a physical trespass.

But although Alito, Ginsburg, Breyer, and Kagan obviously wanted Scalia to go further, it's encouraging that the justices are no longer arguing about *whether* to regulate virtual surveillance in public but instead about how best to protect privacy in light of new technologies. And as Senator Leahy points out, Congress can and should respond to the Court's opinion by imposing legislative restrictions on GPS tracking. In particular, the Geolocation Privacy and Surveillance Act, co-sponsored by Sen. Ron Wyden (D-OR) and Rep. Josh Chaffetz (R-UT) is the most promising way to prevent the government from demanding unlimited access to geolocation information stored by private companies. By passing the GPS Act by bipartisan majorities, the House and Senate can invoke as a model the impressive bipartisan performance of the Roberts Court.

> *"By failing to address the privacy ramifications of . . . new technologies, the Court has done little to curb the government's ceaseless, suspicionless surveillance of innocent Americans."*

The Supreme Court's Recent Decision in the Privacy Case *US v. Jones* Does Not Go Far Enough

John W. Whitehead

In the following viewpoint, John W. Whitehead argues that the US Supreme Court's decision in United States v. Jones *(2012) did not go far enough, failing to incorporate into the right to privacy a recognition that new technologies do not require physical intrusion. He gives several examples of surveillance technologies not covered by the Court's ruling. He concludes that government must be prohibited from using these new technologies for citizen surveillance, calling for a technological bill of rights. Whitehead is an attorney, author, and founder of the Rutherford Institute, a nonprofit civil liberties and human rights organization.*

As you read, consider the following questions:
1. According to Whitehead, what operable word throughout the majority opinion in *United States v. Jones* shows it did not go far enough?
2. In what manner can cell phones be used for government surveillance, according to the author?
3. Whitehead charges that the Court's ruling in *Jones* has ensured that core values of which constitutional amendment will continue to be undermined?

In a unanimous 9–0 ruling in *United States v. Jones* [2012], the U.S. Supreme Court has declared that police must get a search warrant before using GPS [global positioning system] technology to track criminal suspects. But what does this ruling, hailed as a victory by privacy advocates, really mean for the future of privacy and the Fourth Amendment?

An Insufficient Ruling

While the Court rightly recognized that the government's *physical* attachment of a GPS device to Antoine Jones' vehicle for the purpose of tracking Jones' movements constitutes a search under the Fourth Amendment, a careful reading of the Court's opinion, written by Justice Antonin Scalia, shows that the battle over our privacy rights is far from over.

Given that the operable word throughout the ruling is "physical," the ruling does not go far enough. The Court should have clearly delineated the boundaries of permissible surveillance within the context of rapidly evolving technologies and reestablishing the vitality of the Fourth Amendment. Instead, the justices relied on an "18th-century guarantee against un-reasonable searches, which we believe must provide *at a minimum* the degree of protection it afforded when it was adopted."

As Justice Samuel Alito recognizes in his concurring judgment, physical intrusion is now unnecessary to many forms of invasive surveillance. The government's arsenal of surveillance technologies now includes a multitude of devices which enable it to comprehensively monitor an individual's private life without necessarily introducing the type of *physical* intrusion into his person or property covered by the ruling. Thus, by failing to address the privacy ramifications of these new technologies, the Court has done little to curb the government's ceaseless, suspicionless surveillance of innocent Americans.

The New Surveillance Technologies

In the spirit of the Court's ruling in *US v. Jones*, the following surveillance technologies, now available to law enforcement, would not require government officials to engage in a physical trespass of one's property in order to engage in a search:

Drones—pilotless, remote-controlled aircraft that have been used extensively in Iraq, Afghanistan and Pakistan—are being used increasingly domestically by law enforcement. Law enforcement officials promise to use drones to locate missing children and hunt illegal marijuana plants, but under many states' proposed rules, they could also be used to track citizens and closely monitor individuals based on the mere suspicions of law enforcement officers. The precision with which drones can detect intimate activity is remarkable. For instance, a drone can tell whether a hiker eight miles away is carrying a backpack.

Surveillance cameras are an ever-growing presence in American cities. A member of the surveillance camera industry states that, "pretty soon, security cameras will be like smoke detectors: They'll be everywhere." The cameras, installed on office buildings, banks, stores, and private establishments, open the door to suspicionless monitoring of innocent individuals that chill the exercise of First Amendment rights. For example, the New York Police Department has adopted the practice of videotaping individuals engaged in lawful public demonstrations.

"The World of Surveillance," cartoon by Wilfred Hildonen. www.cartoonstock.com.

The government also uses traffic cameras as a form of visual surveillance to track individuals as they move about a city. In some areas, a network of traffic cameras provides a comprehensive view of the streets. In 2009, Chicago had 1,500 cameras set up throughout the city and actively used them to track persons of interest.

Smart dust devices are tiny wireless microelectromechanical sensors (MEMS) that can detect light and movement. These "motes" could eventually be as tiny as a grain of sand, but will still be capable of gathering massive amounts of data, running computations and communicating that information using two-way band radio between motes as far as 1,000 feet away. The goal for researchers is to reduce these chips from their current size of 5 mm to a size of 1 mm per side. In the near future law enforcement officials will be able to use these tiny devices to maintain covert surveillance operations on unsuspecting citizens.

RFIDs, Radio Frequency Identifications, have the ability to contain or transmit information wirelessly using radio waves. These devices can be as small as a grain of rice and can be attached to virtually anything, from a piece of clothing to a vehicle. If manufacturers and other distributors of clothing, personal electronics, and other items begin to tag their products with RFID, any law enforcement officer armed with an RFID reader could covertly search an individual without his or her knowledge.

Technology That Collects Personal Information

Cell phones, increasingly, contain tracking chips which enable cellular providers to collect data on and identify the location of the user. The collected geodata is stored on the device, anonymized with a random identification number, and transmitted over an encrypted Wi-Fi network to the cell phone provider. It is reasonable to expect that government will eventually attempt to tap the troves of information maintained by these cellphone providers.

Collection of Wi-Fi Data: Recently, a professor at Stevens Institute of Technology invented for a mere $600 an aerial drone that can spy on even private Wi-Fi networks. The drone the professor created was a mere eighteen inches long. Such a device could be used to detect financial information, personal correspondence, and any other data transmitted over the wireless network. Coupled with the visual component of the aerial drones, these drones will be capable of detecting almost all intimate or personal activity.

Facial-recognition software is another tool in police forces' surveillance arsenal in which police take a photograph of a person's face, then compare the biometrics to other photographs in a database. Such a system can easily be placed onto the back of a smart phone and only weighs 12.5 ounces. Facial-recognition software is currently being used in conjunction with public surveillance cameras at airports and major public events to spot suspected terrorists or criminals. Cities such as Tampa have attempted to use this technology on busy sidewalks and in public places.

Iris scanners have quickly moved from the realm of science fiction into everyday public use by governments and private businesses. Iris recognition is rarely impeded by contact lenses or eyeglasses, and can work with blind individuals as well. The scanners, which have been used by some American police departments, can scan up to 50 people a minute without requiring the individuals to stop and stand in front of the scanners. The introduction of sophisticated iris scanners in a number of public locations, including train stations, shopping centers, medical centers, and banks in Leon, Mexico, is merely a foreshadowing of what is coming to the U.S. The information gathered from the scanners is sent to a central database that can be used to track any individual's movement throughout the city.

The Need for a Technological Bill of Rights

As this list shows, the current state of technology enables government agents to monitor unsuspecting citizens in virtually any situation. One of the hallmarks of citizenship in a free society is the expectation that one's personal affairs and physical person are inviolable so long as one conforms his or her conduct to the law. Otherwise, we are all suspects in a police state. Any meaningful conception of liberty encompasses freedom from constant and covert government surveillance—whether or not that intrusion is physical or tangible and whether it occurs in public or private. Thus, unchecked technological surveillance is objectionable simply because government has no legitimate authority to covertly monitor the totality of a citizen's daily activities. The root of the problem is not that government is doing something inherently harmful, but rather that government is doing something it has no lawful basis to be doing.

Unfortunately, by failing to establish a Fourth Amendment framework that includes protection against pervasive electronic spying methods that are physically unintrusive and monitor a person's activities in public, the Court has ensured that the core values within the Fourth Amendment will continue to be fundamentally undermined. New technologies which enable the radical expansion of police surveillance operations require correspondingly robust legal frameworks in order to maintain the scope of freedom from authoritarian oversight envisioned by the Framers.

Obviously, the new era of technology, one that was completely unimaginable to the men who drafted the Constitution and the Bill of Rights, requires an updated legal code to enshrine the right to privacy. The courts, first of all, must interpret the Fourth Amendment protection against unreasonable search and seizure as a check against GPS technology as well as future technologies which threaten privacy. Second, as Justice Alito recognized, "the best solution to privacy concerns may be legislative. A legislative body is well situated to gauge changing public attitudes, to draw detailed lines, and to balance privacy and public safety in a comprehensive way." I would take that one step further and propose that Congress enact a technological Bill of Rights to protect us from the long arm of the surveillance state. This would provide needed guidance to law enforcement agencies, quell litigation, protect civil liberties including cherished First Amendment rights, and ensure the viability of the Fourth Amendment even at the dawn of a new age of surveillance technology.

> *"There are those who once again want
> to implement a wall that would place
> civil liberties ahead of national security
> and Americans' safety."*

Security Requires That Civil Liberties, Including Privacy, Not Be Absolute

Elise Cooper

In the following viewpoint, Elise Cooper argues that it is a mistake to privilege civil liberties above national security. Cooper describes a metaphorical wall built to prevent law enforcement from sharing information with intelligence in an attempt to protect civil liberties, including privacy. In the interest of security, she claims, the wall was eradicated after 9/11. However, she expresses concern that a resurgence of the wall is once again threatening national security. Cooper is a columnist and assistant publicist.

As you read, consider the following questions:

    1. According to the author, what act was passed in response to the intelligence scandals of the mid-1970s?

Elise Cooper, "The 'Wall' Continues to Hamstring Anti-Terror Activities," *American Thinker*, November 9, 2012. Copyright © 2012 by American Thinker. All rights reserved. Reproduced by permission.

2. The author expresses concern that a wall is being built by privacy groups in what realm of possible future warfare?

3. What political entity is refusing to share passenger information with the United States, according to Cooper?

The 9/11 attacks occurred in part because the intelligence on terrorist dangers was suppressed as a result of a policy known as "the wall." This policy prevented the intelligence and prosecution sides from sharing information. On April 13, 2004, Attorney General [John] Ashcroft told the 9/11 Commission that the "wall" between law enforcement and intelligence was responsible for many of the failures.

The Wall Between Law Enforcement and Intelligence

FISA (Foreign Intelligence Surveillance Act) was brought into existence during the [Jimmy] Carter administration in response to the intelligence scandals of the mid-1970s because of the assumption that the intelligence agencies acted improperly. A set of rules was written for intelligence-gathering in the states to make sure wiretaps and surveillance were carried out in accordance with the law. The rules that apply to law enforcement wiretaps were not appropriate for intelligence wiretaps, which require more flexibility.

The idea behind FISA was that the contact between prosecutors and intelligence wiretaps should be kept to a minimum to prevent American liberties from being eroded. The "wall" would keep the prosecution side and the intelligence side separate. All that could be given to the prosecutors was a tip to start an investigation, but not the details of the intelligence. Prior to 9/11, there were warning signs which Stewart Baker, former assistant secretary for homeland security, called a "failure of imagination. Frances Townsend [who spearheaded the FISA intelligence investigations] tried to break down the wall. She tried to make a lot of changes for the good. She was more open-minded and aggressive." Unfortunately, she was dismissed because of her efforts.

After 9/11, "the wall" was formally eradicated by Congress and the Court of Appeals. However, there are still barriers today, walls that are less pronounced. Baker, who recently wrote the book *Skating on Stilts*, notes that

> even after the 9/11 attack people are suspicious of limits to their civil liberties, are pushing back the pendulum in the other direction, and still have the assumption that the threats have been overstated by government agencies that want to yield more power.

Civil Liberties vs. Security

One example is the ACLU [American Civil Liberties Union] lawsuit asking a federal judge to halt an alleged [Barack] Obama administration plan to kill an American citizen cleric. The cleric is living in Yemen and encourages radicalized Americans to initiate terrorist attacks. The suit alleges that the targeted-killing program violates Anwar al-Awlaki's Fourth Amendment right to be free from unreasonable seizure and his Fifth Amendment right not to be deprived of life without due process. There are those who once again want to implement a wall that would place civil liberties ahead of national security and Americans' safety.

Will cyber warfare be the next area of attack? A wall is being built by the privacy groups and the cyber industry because they do not want any form of regulation. Jim Roth, the former New York Chief Division Council of the FBI who was heavily involved in FISA, wants a balance between national security concerns and the internet. He strongly believes that "the side of national security must win during any emergency since our First Amendment rights are not absolute. You can't yell fire in a movie theatre."

America's cyber infrastructure is not well-protected, and it is possible that an attack would bring this nation to its knees. Baker says the cyber-industrial complex does not want to be regulated, so they play off the civil liberties side, claiming that any regulation, even for security measures, would be a civil liberties disaster. Townsend suggests that this cyber wall can be easily demolished if the government changes its perspective. According to Townsend, the government must initiate a private-public partnership since so much of the "intellectual capital with cyber resides in the private sector. The government should change its thinking process and involve the private sector in the policy generated process not after."

The Need for Balance

Another wall has been created by the European Union. They refuse to share any passenger name recognition data because of their perceived threat to civil liberties. The Europeans are attempting to limit the kind of information that is passed on to the U.S. and will allow only Homeland Security to use it. They do not want it passed on to other agencies, such as the FBI. Baker emphasized that the data is needed to improve passenger screening. For example, if a European flies to Pakistan and back to Europe and then some time later flies to the U.S., the first leg of the trip is not passed on; thus, the Europeans are preventing the U.S. from connecting the dots. According to Baker, "The EU will forbid airlines from giving the information to the third country (the U.S.) if the third country doesn't dance to their tune: the European supervision on privacy issues." To break down this wall, Baker proposes that the U.S. might consider talking directly with individual countries and bypassing the EU. He also believes that the U.S. might want to limit the "sharing of terrorism data with countries that restrict our ability to collect such data. It makes no sense that the Europeans are trying to limit the kind of information needed to make sure people don't get on planes and blow themselves up over the U.S."

All interviewed agree that there must be an honest dialogue sooner rather than later. Michael Hayden, the former CIA [Central Intelligence Agency] Director, feels that the balance between the concerns of the civil libertarians and national security "should lead to an honest conversation of what do we want to do and what don't we want to do. Some of the decisions of what not to do will increase the risk."

*"It's worth reminding ourselves . . .
that surrendering privacy does
not automatically make us more
secure—that systems of surveillance
can themselves be a major source of
insecurity."*

Surveillance Can't Make Us Secure

Julian Sanchez

*In the following viewpoint, Julian Sanchez argues that the growth
in government surveillance in recent years actually poses security
risks, rather than increasing national security. Sanchez claims that
surveillance systems themselves have become a target of hackers
and spies. He contends that telecommunications companies have
designed their systems for government surveillance, thereby col-
lecting volumes of information and increasing the appetite for surveillance by government. Sanchez is a research fellow at the Cato
Institute and a contributing editor for* Reason *magazine.*

As you read, consider the following questions:

1. According to Sanchez, what events led to Secretary of
   State Hillary Clinton's urging to challenge government
   censorship and surveillance?

2. What law required telephone providers to build networks ready-made for easy and automatic wiretapping, according to the author?
3. According to Sanchez, giant wireless providers get approximately how many law enforcement requests for information each year?

In a major speech[1] on Internet freedom last week, Secretary of State Hillary Clinton urged American tech companies to "take a proactive role in challenging foreign governments' demands for censorship and surveillance." Her call to action followed a series of dazzlingly sophisticated cyberattacks[2] against online giant Google and more than thirty other major technology companies, believed to originate in the People's Republic of China. Few observers have found the Chinese government's staunch denials[3] of involvement persuasive— but the attacks should also spur our own government to review the ways our burgeoning surveillance state has made us more vulnerable.

The Google hackers appear to have been interested in, among other things, gathering information about Chinese dissidents and human rights activists—and they evidently succeeded in obtaining account information and e-mail subject lines for a number of Gmail users. While Google is understandably reluctant to go into detail about the mechanics of the breach, a source at the company told *ComputerWorld*[4] "they apparently were able to access a system used to help Google comply with [US] search warrants by providing data on Google users." In other words, a portal set up to help the American government catch criminals may have proved just as handy at helping the Chinese government find dissidents.

In a way, the hackers' strategy makes perfect sense. Communications networks are generally designed to restrict outside access to their users' private information. But the goal of government surveillance is to create a breach-by-design, a deliberate back-door into otherwise carefully secured systems. The appeal to an intruder is obvious: Why waste time with retail hacking of many individual targets when you can break into the network itself and spy wholesale?

The Google hackers are scarcely the first to exploit such security holes. In the summer of 2004, unknown intruders managed to activate wiretapping software[5] embedded in the systems of Greece's largest cellular carrier. For ten months, the hackers eavesdropped on the cellphone calls of more than 100 prominent citizens—including the prime minister, opposition members of parliament, and high cabinet officials.

It's hard to know just how many other such instances there are, because Google's decision to go public is quite unusual: companies typically have no incentive to spook customers (or invite hackers) by announcing a security breach. But the little we know about the existing surveillance infrastructure does not inspire great confidence.

Consider the FBI's Digital Collection System Network, or DCSNet. Via a set of dedicated, encrypted lines plugged directly into the nation's telecom hubs, DCSNet[6] is designed to allow authorized law enforcement agents to initiate a wiretap or gather information with point-and-click simplicity. Yet a 2003 internal audit, released several years later under a freedom-of-information request, found a slew of problems in the system's setup that appalled security experts. Designed with external threats in mind, it had few safeguards against an attack assisted by a Robert Hanssen–style accomplice on the inside. We can hope those problems have been resolved by now. But if new vulnerabilities are routinely discovered in programs used by millions, there's little reason to hope that bespoke spying software can be rendered airtight.

Of even greater concern, though, are the ways the government has encouraged myriad private telecoms and Internet providers to design for breach.

The most obvious means by which this is happening is direct legal pressure. State-sanctioned eavesdroppers have always been able to demand access to existing telecommunications infrastructure. But the Communications Assistance for Law Enforcement Act of 1994 went further, requiring telephone providers to begin building networks ready-made for easy and automatic wiretapping. Federal regulators recently expanded that requirement to cover broadband and many voice-over-Internet providers. The proposed SAFETY Act of 2009 would compound the security risk by requiring Internet providers to retain users' traffic logs for at least two years, just in case law enforcement should need to browse through them.

A less obvious, but perhaps more serious factor is the sheer volume of surveillance the government now engages in. If government data caches contain vast quantities of information unrelated to narrow criminal investigations—routinely gathered in the early phases of an investigation to identify likely targets—attackers will have much greater incentive to expend time and resources on compromising them. The FBI's database now contains billions of records from a plethora of public and private sources, much of it gathered in the course of broad, preliminary efforts to determine who merits further investigation. The sweeping, programmatic NSA surveillance authorized by the FISA Amendments Act of 2008 has reportedly captured e-mails from the likes of former President Bill Clinton.

The volume of requests from both federal and state law enforcement has also put pressure on telecoms to automate their processes for complying with government information requests. In a leaked recording[7] from the secretive ISS world surveillance conference held back in October, Sprint/Nextel's head of surveillance described how the company's L-Site portal was making it possible to deal with the ballooning demand for information:

> My major concern is the volume of requests. We have a lot of things that are automated, but that's just scratching the

surface. . . . Like with our GPS tool. We turned it on—the web interface for law enforcement—about one year ago last month, and we just passed 8 million requests. So there is no way on earth my team could have handled 8 million requests from law enforcement, just for GPS alone. So the [L-Site portal] has just really caught on fire with law enforcement. They also love that it is extremely inexpensive to operate and easy, so, just the sheer volume of requests . . . They anticipate us automating other features, and I just don't know how we'll handle the millions and millions of requests that are going to come in.

Behold the vicious cycle. Weakened statutory standards have made it easier and more attractive for intelligence and law enforcement agencies to seek information from providers. On top of the thousands of wiretap and so-called "pen/trap" orders approved each year, there are *tens* of thousands of National Security Letters and subpoenas. At the ISS world conference, a representative of Cricket, one of the smaller wireless providers, estimated that her company gets 200 law enforcement requests per day, all told; giants like Verizon[8] have said they receive "tens of thousands" annually. (Those represent distinct legal demands for information; Sprint's "8 million" refers to individual electronic requests for updates on a target's location.)

Telecoms respond to the crush of requests by building a faster, more seamless, more user-friendly process for dealing with those requests—further increasing the appeal of such tools to law enforcement. Unfortunately, insecurity loves company: more information flowing to more legitimate users is that much more difficult to lock down effectively. Later in his conference, the Sprint representative at the ISS World conference speculated that someone who mocked up a phony legal request and faxed it to a random telecom would have a good chance of getting it answered. The recipients just can't thoroughly vet every request they get.

We've gotten so used to the "privacy/security tradeoff" that it's worth reminding ourselves, every now and again, that surrendering privacy does not automatically make us more secure—that systems of surveillance can themselves be a major source of *in*security. Hillary Clinton is absolutely right that tech companies seeking to protect Internet freedom should begin "challenging foreign governments' demands for censorship and surveillance." But her entreaty contains precisely one word too many.

Notes

1. http://www.state.gov/secretary/rm/2010/01/135519.htm
2. http://googlepublicpolicy.blogspot.com/2010/01/new-approach-to-%20china.html
3. http://abcnews.go.com/International/china-google-hacking-claims-%20groundless/story?id=9654628
4. http://www.computerworld.com/s/article/9144221/%20Google_attack_part_of_widespread_spying_effort
5. http://spectrum.ieee.org/telecom/security/the-athens-affair
6. http://www.wired.com/politics/security/news/2007/08/wiretap
7. http://paranoia.dubfire.net/2009/12/8-million-reasons-for-real-%20surveillance.html
8. http://files.cloudprivacy.net/verizon-price-list-letter.PDF

| "*Americans value privacy and expect protection from intrusions by both private and governmental actors.*"

New Legislation Is Needed to Protect Privacy on the Internet

The Obama Administration

In the following viewpoint, the administration of Barack Obama argues that the growth in networked technologies has created the need for stronger privacy protections on the Internet. The Obama administration contends that preserving trust online is important for commerce and for realizing the full social and cultural benefits of the Internet. The Obama administration proposes a new consumer data privacy framework. The administration of President Barack Obama assumed office on January 20, 2009.

As you read, consider the following questions:

1. According to the authors, online retail sales in the United States total what amount annually?
2. Does the Obama administration support modifying existing federal statutes or creating new legislation to protect online privacy?

The White House, Barack Obama Administration, "Consumer Data Privacy in a Networked World: A Framework for Protecting Privacy and Promoting Innovation in the Global Digital Economy," February 2012, pp. 5–7.

3. The Obama administration claims that the consumer rights identified in the new consumer data privacy framework are based on what set of principles?

The Internet is integral to economic and social life in the United States and throughout the world. Networked technologies offer individuals nearly limitless ways to express themselves, form social connections, transact business, and organize politically. Networked technologies also spur innovation, enable new business models, and facilitate consumers' and companies' access to information, products, and services markets across the world.

The Need for Strong Privacy Protections

An abundance of data, inexpensive processing power, and increasingly sophisticated analytical techniques drive innovation in our increasingly networked society. Political organizations and candidates for public office build powerful campaigns on data that individuals share about themselves and their political preferences. Data from social networks allows journalists and individuals to report and follow newsworthy events around the world as they unfold. Data plays a key role in the ability of government to stop identity thieves and protect public safety. Researchers use sets of medical data to identify public health issues and probe the causes of human diseases. Network operators use data from communications networks to identify events ranging from a severed fiber optic cable to power outages and the acts of malicious intruders. In addition, personal data fuels an advertising marketplace that brings many online services and sources of content to consumers for free.

Strengthening consumer data privacy protections in the United States is an important Administration priority. Americans value privacy and expect protection from intrusions by both private and governmental actors. Strong privacy protections also

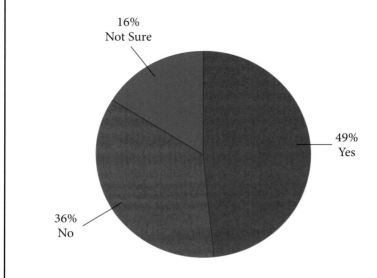

US Public Opinion on the Government's Role in Protecting Online Privacy

"Do you believe government regulators should play a larger role in protecting online consumer privacy?"

16%
Not Sure

49%
Yes

36%
No

TAKEN FROM: Zogby International poll, June 4–7, 2010.

are critical to sustaining the trust that nurtures Internet commerce and fuels innovation. Trust means the companies and technical systems on which we depend meet our expectations for privacy, security, and reliability. In addition, United States leadership in consumer data privacy can help establish more flexible, innovation-enhancing privacy models among our international partners.

The Importance of Preserving Trust

Preserving trust in the Internet economy protects and enhances substantial economic activity. Online retail sales in the United

States total $145 billion annually. New uses of personal data in location services, protected by appropriate privacy and security safeguards, could create important business opportunities. Moreover, the United States is a world leader in exporting cloud computing, location-based services, and other innovative services. To preserve these economic benefits, consumers must continue to trust networked technologies. Strengthening consumer data privacy protections will help to achieve this goal.

Preserving trust also is necessary to realize the full social and cultural benefits of networked technologies. When companies use personal data in ways that are inconsistent with the circumstances under which consumers disclosed the data, however, they may undermine trust. For example, individuals who actively share information with their friends, family, colleagues, and the general public through websites and online social networking sites may not be aware of the ways those services, third parties, and their own associates may use information about them. Unauthorized disclosure of sensitive information can violate individual rights, cause injury or discrimination based on sensitive personal attributes, lead to actions and decisions taken in response to misleading or inaccurate information, and contribute to costly and potentially life-disrupting identity theft. Protecting Americans' privacy by preventing identity theft and prosecuting identity thieves is an important focus for the Administration.

The existing consumer data privacy framework in the United States is flexible and effectively addresses some consumer data privacy challenges in the digital age. This framework consists of industry best practices, FTC [Federal Trade Commission] enforcement, and a network of chief privacy officers and other privacy professionals who develop privacy practices that adapt to changes in technology and business models and create a growing culture of privacy awareness within companies. Much of the personal data used on the Internet, however, is not subject to comprehensive Federal statutory protection, because most Federal data privacy statutes apply only to specific sectors, such as healthcare, education, communications, and financial services or, in the case of online data collection, to children. The Administration believes that filling gaps in the existing framework will promote more consistent responses to privacy concerns across the wide range of environments in which individuals have access to networked technologies and in which a broad array of companies collect and use personal data. The Administration, however, does not recommend modifying the existing Federal statutes that apply to specific sectors unless they set inconsistent standards for related technologies. Instead, the Administration supports legislation that would supplement the existing framework and extend baseline protections to the sectors that existing Federal statutes do not cover.

A New Consumer Data Privacy Framework

The comprehensive consumer data privacy framework . . . will provide clearer protections for consumers. It will also provide greater certainty for companies while promoting innovation and minimizing compliance costs. . . . The framework provides consumers who want to understand and control how personal data flows in the digital economy with better tools to do so. The proposal ensures that companies striving to meet consumers' expectations have more effective ways of engaging consumers and policymakers. This will help companies to determine which personal data practices consumers find unobjectionable and which ones they find invasive. Finally, the Administration's consumer data privacy framework improves our global competitiveness by promoting international policy frameworks that reflect how consumers and companies actually use networked technologies.

As a world leader in Internet innovation, the United States has both the responsibility and incentive to help establish forward-looking privacy policy models that foster innovation and preserve basic privacy rights. The Administration's framework for consumer data privacy offers a path toward achieving these goals. It is based on the following key elements:

- A *Consumer Privacy Bill of Rights*, setting forth individual rights and corresponding obligations of companies in connection with personal data. These consumer rights are based on U.S.-developed and globally recognized Fair Information Practice Principles (FIPPs), articulated in terms that apply to the dynamic environment of the Internet age;

- *Enforceable codes of conduct*, developed through *multi-stakeholder processes*, to form the basis for specifying what the Consumer Privacy Bill of Rights requires in particular business contexts;

- Federal Trade Commission (FTC) *enforcement* of consumers' data privacy rights through its authority to prohibit unfair or deceptive acts or practices; and

- Increasing *global interoperability* between the U.S. consumer data privacy framework and other countries' frameworks, through mutual recognition, the development of codes of conduct through multistakeholder processes, and enforcement cooperation can reduce barriers to the flow of information.

> *"Before we . . . enact invasive laws and regulations . . . let's exercise our right to protect our privacy by using the many online and legal tools already at our fingertips."*

New Legislation Is Not Needed to Protect Privacy on the Internet

John Stephenson

In the following viewpoint, John Stephenson argues that the Obama administration's call for new privacy laws governing the Internet is unnecessary and dangerous. Stephenson claims that the new regulations could limit consumer choice online and place an economic burden on Internet businesses. He contends that existing law, along with privacy protections created by online companies themselves, are sufficient. Stephenson is director of the Communications and Technology Task Force at the American Legislative Exchange Council.

As you read, consider the following questions:

1. The author explains that the Obama administration promises that new privacy laws will keep data safe without doing what?

2. According to a study to which Stephenson refers, how much would government-mandated privacy regulations cost US businesses over five years?

3. The author claims that companies have responded to consumer concerns about privacy by providing tools that protect privacy in what kinds of ways?

Privacy is one of our most cherished values, especially in this increasingly connected world. There is no question that we all want to be able to protect ourselves from harms or intrusions into our lives by the government or marketers. Some argue for new, invasive laws and government mandates to protect our privacy. But why not use the laws and sophisticated technologies currently at our disposal to exercise our freedom to protect our privacy?

The Call for Government Regulation

In January [2012] the Obama administration released its long-awaited proposal outlining a new role for the federal government in policing the Internet. The white paper, "Consumer Data Privacy in a Networked World: A Framework for Protecting Privacy and Innovation in the Global Digital Economy," calls for new privacy laws the administration says will enable people to keep their data safe without compromising the dynamic and growing online economy.

That is certainly a noble goal, but the reality behind the rhetoric deserves careful scrutiny.

Although couched in the soaring language of our constitutionally guaranteed freedoms, the administration's white paper seeks extensive new government regulation of the Internet to address what Berin Szoka and Larry Downes, both of Tech Freedom, call "little more than the growing pains of a vibrant emerging economy."

A Hazard of Privacy Regulation

Privacy regulation that works "too well" would give people more privacy than is optimal, making consumers worse off overall. Consumers have interests not just in privacy, but also in publicity, access to content, customization, convenience, low prices, and so on. Many of these interests are in tension with privacy, and giving consumers privacy at the cost of other things they prefer is not a good outcome.

The dominant model for producing Internet content—all the interaction, commentary, news, imagery, and entertainment that has the Internet thriving—is advertising support. Many of the most popular services and platforms are "free" because they host advertisements directed at their visitors and users. Part of the reason they can support themselves with advertising is because they have good information about users that allow ads to be appropriately targeted. It is a fact that well-targeted ads are more valuable than less-well-targeted ads.

This is important to note: Most web-based businesses do not "sell" information about their users. In targeted online advertising, the business model is generally to sell advertisers access to people ("eyeballs") based on their demographics. It is not to sell individuals' personal and contact info. Doing the latter would undercut the advertising business model and the profitability of the web sites carrying the advertising.

If privacy regulation "blinded" sites and platforms to relevant information about their visitors, the advertising-supported model for Internet content would likely be degraded. Consumers would be worse off—entombed by an excess of privacy when their preferences would be to have more content and more interaction than regulation allows advertising to support.

Jim Harper, Congressional Testimony,
July 27, 2010.

The Danger of New Regulation

The white paper aims for government-driven accountability mandates and data-collection strictures—not to mention yet-to-be-developed "one touch, one click" technologies for controlling the use of personal information—that threaten to undermine a working and growing model for business on the Internet. Moreover, these proposed new laws could undermine the freedom that has long been the hallmark of the Internet by sharply limiting personal choice in the goods and services consumers can enjoy.

A study by NetChoice, a trade association representing e-commerce and Internet companies, estimates government-mandated privacy regulations could cost U.S. companies $33 billion over five years. To some of the administration's allies this may seem inconsequential, but imposing this burden on businesses could have unintended consequences for everyone who values their choices online. Although large companies might be able to absorb these new regulatory and compliance costs, smaller companies and startups like the new and popular Web site Pinterest, one of the few bright spots in the economy, could be forced to shut down or flee the country, thereby limiting consumer choices.

American consumers are also deeply skeptical that more regulation of the Internet will help. In a recent Zogby poll commissioned by the National Taxpayers Union, 76 percent agreed that "[m]ore government involvement and regulation will make the Internet worse for consumers," while only 8 percent believe regulation "will make the Internet better for consumers."

The Tools That Already Exist

Ironically, much of what the administration hopes to achieve through the top-down approaches outlined in the white paper already is easily available to consumers. An entire body of law, from the Constitution's Fourth Amendment to state consumer-protection laws, has been developed and proven to be effective in protecting consumers from wrongdoers.

Moreover, online companies understand consumers are concerned about their privacy. These companies have responded by providing sophisticated, easy-to-use tools to prevent tracking, block spam, or delete the list of Web pages visited. Upon a cursory glance at my Web-based email account, I can find a link called "Terms and Privacy." A click on the link takes me to a page that lists the privacy policy, links to key terms, a link to contact the company with questions, and a link to tools where I can limit how my data is used.

A single click on my Facebook page reveals a similar menu of privacy controls. All it took for me to find the privacy notice and many options on Microsoft's Bing search engine was to scroll to the bottom of the page. Google even has how-to videos showing you how to adjust your privacy settings.

Clearly, privacy control and information are literally at our fingertips, and they are there not because of a government mandate but because companies respond to consumer demands. Dynamic market forces have encouraged Internet-based firms to alter how they collect and use data and will continue to do so. Those who respond quickly to privacy concerns will earn loyalty, while those who don't lose their customer base.

Before we spend another two years trying to enact invasive laws and regulations called for in a government white paper —that may do more harm than good while limiting users' choices—let's exercise our right to protect our privacy by using the many online and legal tools already at our fingertips.

Periodical and Internet Sources Bibliography

The following articles have been selected to supplement the diverse views presented in this chapter.

Arnold Ahlert	"Privacy v. Technology," *FrontPage*, March 9, 2012. www.frontpagemag.com.
Nat Hentoff	"We Can't Hide from the National Security Agency," Cato Institute, April 11, 2012. www.cato.org.
Cecilia King	"Parting with Privacy with a Quick Click," *Washington Post*, May 8, 2011.
Monica Yant Kinney	"Another Pin in the Privacy Balloon," *Philadelphia Inquirer*, February 28, 2010.
Adam Serwer	"Where Is the Right to Privacy? It Doesn't Exist If You're a Muslim," *Mother Jones*, June 6, 2012.
Daniel J. Solove	"Why 'Security' Keeps Winning Out over Privacy," *Salon*, May 31, 2011. www.salon.com.
Jacob Sullum	"How GPS Tracking Threatens Privacy," *Reason*, January 25, 2012.
John Villasenor	"Why the Supreme Court GPS Decision Won't Stop Warrantless Digital Surveillance," *Scientific American*, January 25, 2012.
Patricia J. Williams	"Do We Have Any Right to Privacy Outside Our Homes?," *The Nation*, December 12, 2011.
John Yoo	"Why We Endorsed Warrantless Wiretaps," *Wall Street Journal*, July 16, 2009.

For Further Discussion

Chapter 1

1. Joyce Arthur uses the example of violence against abortion providers to support her view that hate speech can incite violence. How would Jacob Mchangama respond to Arthur's assertion that people who express hate should be at least partially liable for the actions of those who commit acts of violence?

2. Steve Simpson contends that corporations are just groups of individuals and ought to have the same kind of free speech rights as any other group of individuals. What objection does Jeffrey D. Clements raise to this line of reasoning? Who makes the better argument in your opinion? Why?

Chapter 2

1. Explain the contrasting views that Garrett Epps and Antony Barone Kolenc give of the views of the Founding Fathers on separation of church and state. Why is this issue relevant?

2. Focusing on the specific example given by Newt Gingrich of what he contends is antireligious judicial extremism, how might David Niose argue that such an example constitutes government neutrality? What might Niose claim constitutes real antireligion bias in that realm?

Chapter 3

1. Charles D. Stimson and Glenn Greenwald disagree about the wisdom of the passage of section 1021 of the 2012 National Defense Authorization Act. They also disagree about what section 1021 actually accomplishes. Name at least one point of disagreement regarding how the law works. Give your opinion on this issue now that you have read both sides.

2. Jacqueline Stevens claims that immigration courts are wrongly deporting US citizens. How, then, might Stevens respond to W.D. Reasoner's call for more expedited removals?

Chapter 4

1. Jeffrey Rosen and John W. Whitehead have different degrees of enthusiasm regarding the US Supreme Court's 2012 decision in *United States v. Jones*. What is one point of agreement between the two?

2. Julian Sanchez argues that existing surveillance structures are themselves vulnerable to hackers and spies, creating less security. How do you think Elise Cooper would respond to Sanchez's worry?

3. Both the Obama Administration and John Stephenson use concern for the survival of businesses in their arguments, but arrive at contradictory conclusions. Can both of their concerns be legitimate? Why or why not?

Organizations to Contact

The editors have compiled the following list of organizations concerned with the issues debated in this book. The descriptions are derived from materials provided by the organizations. All have publications or information available for interested readers. The list was compiled on the date of publication of the present volume; names, addresses, phone and fax numbers, and e-mail and Internet addresses may change. Be aware that many organizations take several weeks or longer to respond to inquiries, so allow as much time as possible.

Alliance Defense Fund (ADF)
15100 N. 90th Street
Scottsdale, AZ 85260
(480) 444-0020 • fax: (480) 444-0028
website: www.alliancedefensefund.org

The Alliance Defense Fund is a Christian organization that works to defend religious freedom. It provides legal defense for cases involving religious freedom, the sanctity of life, marriage, and the family. ADF publishes several books, brochures, and pamphlets, including "The Truth About Student Rights."

American Center for Law and Justice (ACLJ)
PO Box 90555
Washington, DC 20090-0555
(800) 296-4529
website: www.aclj.org

The American Center for Law and Justice is dedicated to protecting religious and constitutional freedoms. It has participated in numerous cases before the US Supreme Court, federal courts of appeals, federal district courts, and various state courts regarding freedom of religion and freedom of speech. The ACLJ has numerous memos and position papers available on its website, including, "Protecting the Rights of Students."

American Civil Liberties Union (ACLU)
125 Broad Street, 18th Floor
New York, NY 10004
(212) 549-2500
e-mail: infoaclu@aclu.org
website: www.aclu.org

The American Civil Liberties Union is a national organization that works to defend Americans' civil rights as guaranteed in the US Constitution. It works in courts, legislatures, and communities to defend First Amendment rights, the right to equal protection under the law, the right to due process of law, and the right to privacy. The ACLU publishes the semiannual newsletter *Civil Liberties Alert*, as well as briefing papers, including the report "Locking Up Our Children."

American Jewish Congress
115 E. 57th Street, Suite 11
New York, NY 10022
(212) 879-4500 • fax: (212) 758-1633
e-mail: contact@ajcongress.org
website: www.ajcongress.org

The American Jewish Congress is an association of Jewish Americans organized to defend Jewish interests at home and abroad. The American Jewish Congress engages in public policy advocacy— using diplomacy, legislation, and the courts—to defend religious freedom in the United States. The American Jewish Congress has several publications available on its website, including "Religion and the Public Schools: A Summary of the Law."

American Library Association (ALA)
50 E. Huron Street
Chicago, IL 60611

(800) 545-2433 • fax: (312) 440-9374
e-mail: ala@ala.org
website: www.ala.org

The American Library Association is the nation's primary professional organization for librarians. It provides leadership for the development, promotion, and improvement of library services and librarianship in order to enhance learning and ensure access to information for all. The ALA publishes the *Newsletter on Intellectual Freedom* online, the only journal that reports attempts to remove materials from school and library shelves across the country.

Americans United for Separation of Church and State

1301 K Street NW, Suite 850, East Tower
Washington, DC 20005
(202) 466-3234 • fax: (202) 466-2587
e-mail: americansunited@au.org
website: www.au.org

Americans United for Separation of Church and State is a nonprofit educational organization dedicated to preserving the constitutional principle of church-state separation. It works to defend religious liberty in Congress and state legislatures, aiming to ensure that new legislation and policy protect church-state separation. The organization publishes several books and pamphlets, including *Religion in the Public Schools: A Road Map for Avoiding Lawsuits and Respecting Parents' Legal Rights*.

Becket Fund for Religious Liberty

3000 K Street NW, Suite 220
Washington, DC 20007
(202) 955-0095 • fax: (202) 955-0090
website: www.becketfund.org

The Becket Fund for Religious Liberty is a public-interest law firm protecting the free expression of all religious traditions. The

Becket Fund operates in three arenas: the courts of law (litigation), the court of public opinion (media), and in the academy (scholarship). On its website, the Becket Fund has information about cases in which it has participated, which include cases aimed at protecting private religious schools from discrimination and those aimed at preserving a legitimate role for religious discourse and expression in public schools.

Center for Campus Free Speech
328 S. Jefferson Street, Suite 620
Chicago, IL 60661
(312) 544-4438
e-mail: center@campusspeech.org
website: www.campusspeech.org

The Center for Campus Free Speech was created by students, faculty, administrators, and others to protect and promote free speech on university campuses. The center acts as a clearinghouse of information; provides specialized support to campuses; and connects concerned educators, administrators, lawyers, and students into a national network. The center publishes a variety of reports and papers supporting free speech on campus, including "Manufactured Controversy."

Center for Public Education
1680 Duke Street
Alexandria, VA 22314
(703) 838-6722 • fax: (703) 548-5613
e-mail: centerforpubliced@nsba.org
website: www.centerforpubliceducation.org

The Center for Public Education is a resource center set up by the National School Boards Association (NSBA). The center works to provide information about public education, leading to better understanding of schools, more community involvement, and better decision making by school leaders on behalf of all students in their classrooms. Among the many publications available on the center's website is "Free Speech and Public Schools."

Committee to Protect Journalists (CPJ)
330 Seventh Ave., 11th Floor
New York, NY 10001
(212) 465-1004 • fax: (212) 465-9568
e-mail: info@cpj.org
website: www.cpj.org

CPJ is an independent, nonprofit organization that works to promote freedom of the press worldwide by defending the rights of journalists to report the news without fear of reprisal. CPJ publicly reveals abuses against the press, warns journalists and news organizations where attacks on journalistic freedom are occurring, organizes vigorous public protests, and works through diplomatic channels to effect change. CPJ publishes articles and news releases, special reports, and Attacks on the Press, an annual survey of freedom of the press around the world.

Electronic Frontier Foundation (EFF)
54 Shotwell Street
San Francisco, CA 94110-1914
(415) 436-9333 • fax: (415) 436-9993
e-mail: information@eff.org
website: www.eff.org

EFF works to promote the public interest in critical battles affecting digital rights, defending free speech, privacy, innovation, and consumer rights. It provides legal assistance in cases where it believes it can help shape the law. EFF publishes a newsletter and reports, including "New Agreement Between the United States and Europe Will Compromise the Privacy Rights of International Travelers."

Electronic Privacy Information Center (EPIC)
1718 Connecticut Ave. NW, Suite 200
Washington, DC 20009
(202) 483-1140 • fax: (202) 483-1248
website: www.epic.org

The Electronic Privacy Information Center is a public-interest research center devoted to protecting privacy, the First Amendment, and constitutional values in the electronic age. EPIC publishes reports and books about privacy, open government, free speech, and other important civil liberties topics, as well as annual reports and the *EPIC Alert*, an online newsletter.

First Amendment Coalition
534 Fourth Street, Suite B
San Rafael, CA 94901
(415) 460-5060 • fax: (415) 460-5155
website: www.firstamendmentcoalition.org

The First Amendment Coalition is a nonprofit public interest organization dedicated to advancing free speech, more open and accountable government, and public participation in civic affairs. The coalition offers free legal consultations, engages in litigation, offers educational programs, and engages in public advocacy. Its website contains First Amendment news and opinion, as well as a searchable database from its legal hotline information service, Asked & Answered.

Freedom Forum
555 Pennsylvania Ave. NW
Washington, DC 20001
(202) 292-6100
e-mail: news@freedomforum.org
website: www.freedomforum.org

The Freedom Forum is a nonpartisan foundation dedicated to free press, free speech, and free spirit for all people. The forum's First Amendment Center (www.firstamendmentcenter .org) works to preserve and protect First Amendment freedoms through information and education. It publishes the annual report "State of the First Amendment," as well as numerous other publications, including "The Silencing of Student Voices."

Freedom from Religion Foundation
PO Box 750
Madison, WI 53701
(608) 256-8900
e-mail: info@ffrf.org
website: www.ffrf.org

The Freedom from Religion Foundation is an educational group working for the separation of state and church. Its purposes are to promote that constitutional principle and to educate the public on matters relating to nontheism. It publishes the newspaper *Freethought Today*, as well as several books and brochures, such as "The Case Against School Prayer."

Freedom House
1301 Connecticut Ave. NW, Floor 6
Washington, DC 20036
(202) 296-5101 • fax: (202) 293-2840
e-mail: info@freedomhouse.org
website: www.freedomhouse.org

Freedom House is an independent watchdog organization that supports the expansion of freedom around the world. It supports democratic change, monitors freedom, and advocates for democracy and human rights. Annually, Freedom House publishes the results of its Freedom in the World survey, the *Freedom of the Press* index, and the *Freedom on the Net* report.

National Coalition Against Censorship (NCAC)
275 Seventh Ave., Suite 1504
New York, NY 10001

(212) 807-6222 • fax: (212) 807-6245
e-mail: ncac@ncac.org
website: www.ncac.org

The National Coalition Against Censorship is an alliance of fifty-two participating organizations dedicated to protecting free expression and free access to information. It has many projects dedicated to educating the public and protecting free expression, including the Free Expression Policy Project, the Kids' Right to Read Project, The Knowledge Project: Censorship and Science, and the Youth Free Expression Network. Among NCAC's publications is "The First Amendment in Schools."

People for the American Way (PFAW)
2000 M Street NW, Suite 400
Washington, DC 20036
(202) 467-4999
website: www.pfaw.org

People for the American Way is an organization that fights for progressive values: equal rights, freedom of speech, religious liberty, and equal justice under the law for every American. PFAW works to build and nurture communities of support for their values and to equip those communities to promote progressive policies, elect progressive candidates, and hold public officials accountable. Among its publications on the topic of freedom of speech is the report "Back to School with the Religious Right."

Rutherford Institute
PO Box 7482
Charlottesville, VA 22906-7482
(434) 978-3888 • fax: (434) 978-1789
e-mail: staff@rutherford.org
website: www.rutherford.org

The Rutherford Institute is a civil liberties organization that provides legal services in the defense of religious and civil liberties and aims to educate the public on important issues affecting constitutional freedoms. The institute publishes commentary, articles, and books, including the article "The Future Looks Bleak for the First Amendment."

Bibliography of Books

Floyd Abrams

Speaking Freely: Trials of the First Amendment. New York: Penguin, 2006.

William P. Bloss

Under a Watchful Eye: Privacy Rights and Criminal Justice. Santa Barbara, CA: Praeger, 2009.

Michael D. Cicchini

Tried and Convicted: How Police, Prosecutors, and Judges Destroy Our Constitutional Rights. Lanham, MD: Rowman & Littlefield, 2012.

Kenneth Dautrich, David A. Yalof, and Mark Hugo Lopez

The Future of the First Amendment: The Digital Media, Civic Education, and Free Expression Rights in America's High Schools. Lanham, MD: Rowman & Littlefield, 2008.

John C. Domino

Civil Rights and Liberties in the 21st Century. New York: Longman, 2010.

Anne Proffitt Dupre

Speaking Up: The Unintended Costs of Free Speech in Public Schools. Cambridge, MA: Harvard University Press, 2009.

Noah Feldman

Divided by God: America's Church-State Problem—and What We Should Do About It. New York: Farrar, Straus & Giroux, 2006.

Stephen M. Feldman	*Free Expression and Democracy in America: A History*. Chicago: University of Chicago Press, 2008.
C. Welton Gaddy and Barry W. Lynn	*First Freedom First: A Citizen's Guide to Protecting Religious Liberty and the Separation of Church and State*. Boston: Beacon, 2008.
A.C. Grayling	*Liberty in the Age of Terror: A Defence of Civil Liberties and Enlightenment Values*. London: Bloomsbury, 2011.
Glenn Greenwald	*With Liberty and Justice for Some: How the Law Is Used to Destroy Equality and Protect the Powerful*. New York: Metropolitan, 2011.
Shane Harris	*The Watchers: The Rise of America's Surveillance State*. New York: Penguin, 2010.
Susan N. Herman	*Taking Liberties: The War on Terror and the Erosion of American Democracy*. New York: Oxford University Press, 2011.
Steven J. Heyman	*Free Speech and Human Dignity*. New Haven, CT: Yale University Press, 2008.
David L. Hudson	*The Right to Privacy*. New York: Chelsea House, 2010.
Thomas A. Jacobs	*Teens Take It to Court: Young People Who Challenged the Law—and Changed Your Life*. Minneapolis: Free Spirit, 2006.

Emile Lester	*Teaching About Religions: A Democratic Approach for Public Schools.* Ann Arbor: University of Michigan Press, 2011.
Saul Levmore and Martha C. Nussbaum	*The Offensive Internet: Speech, Privacy, and Reputation.* Cambridge, MA: Harvard University Press, 2010.
Anthony Lewis	*Freedom for the Thought That We Hate: A Biography of the First Amendment.* New York: MJF Books, 2011.
Rebecca MacKinnon	*Consent of the Networked: The Worldwide Struggle for Internet Freedom.* New York: Basic, 2012.
Jon L. Mills	*Privacy: The Lost Right.* New York: Oxford University Press, 2008.
Dawn C. Nunziato	*Virtual Freedom: Net Neutrality and Free Speech in the Internet Age.* Stanford, CA: Stanford Law Books, 2009.
Brad O'Leary	*Shut Up, America! The End of Free Speech.* Los Angeles: WND Books, 2009.
David K. Shipler	*Rights at Risk: The Limits of Liberty in Modern America.* New York: Knopf, 2012.
Christopher Slobogin	*Privacy at Risk: The New Government Surveillance and the Fourth Amendment.* Chicago: University of Chicago Press, 2007.

Janet E. Smith	*The Right to Privacy.* San Francisco: Ignatius Press, 2008.
Daniel J. Solove	*The Future of Reputation: Gossip, Rumor, and Privacy on the Internet.* New Haven, CT: Yale University Press, 2008.
R. Murray Thomas	*God in the Classroom: Religion and America's Public Schools.* Westport, CT: Praeger, 2007.
Leigh Ann Wheeler	*How Sex Became a Civil Liberty.* New York: Oxford University Press, 2012.

Index

A

Abortion providers, 23, 31, 32, 187
Abortion rights, 105
ACLU (American Civil Liberties Union), 153, 155, 180, 187, 203
Adams, John, 98–99, 104
Afghanistan, 41, 150
Al Qaeda, 31, 149, 151, 154, 156
Alabama, 115
Alabama, Powell v. (1932), 145
Al-Awlaki, Anwar, 203
Alibhai-Brown, Yasmin, 82–86
Alito, Samuel, 61, 72, 104, 105, 189–193, 195–196, 200
American Bar Association (ABA), 165–166, 179
American Immigration Lawyers Association, 183
Amish, 112
Anglican Church (Church of England), 104, 123
Anonymous threats, 88
Anti-abortion groups, 24, 29–30
Apple (company), 192
Arizona, 177
Arthur, Joyce, 21–32
Articles of Confederation, 99
Ashcroft, John, 202
Atheism, 26, 34, 99, 103, 105, 109, 115
Austin v. Michigan Chamber of Commerce (1990), 51–55, 63, 73
Australia, 36, 37
Authorization for Use of Military Force (AUMF), 149–150, 151, 153–160
Azores, 176

B

Bachmann, Michele, 97
Baker, Stewart, 202–204
Bank of Boston, 79
Barton, David, 97–98
Belgium, 35
Bender's Immigration Bulletin, 180
Bible, 112, 117, 119
Biery, Fred, 133–137
Bill of Rights (US Constitution)
adoption, 14
intent, 124
interpretation, 15–16
student prayer and, 114
Bin Laden, Osama, 156
Bipartisan Campaign Reform Act, 55–59, 71, 77
Blasphemy, 29, 35
Board of Immigration Appeals, 175
Border Patrol, 170, 171
Bosnia-Herzogovina, 23
Boston College Post-Deportation and Human Rights Project, 176
Bowers v. Hardwick, 65
Boyd v. United States (1886), 186, 188n1
Breivik, Anders Behring, 23–24
Breyer, Stephen, 58–60, 190, 193
Britton, John, 31
Bryan, Clifford, 178–179
Buckley v. Valeo (1976), 46–58, 64
Buddhism, 128
Burnham, David, 179
Bush, George W., 57, 108, 150, 154, 156

C

Campaign contributions

corruption of political process
and, 52–53, 57, 66, 79–80
direct contributions, 51, 53
express advocacy and, 55, 60
impartiality of justice and,
77–78
independent expenditures and,
50
issue advocacy and, 54–56, 60
limitations, 48–49
regulation, 46–48
soft money, 56
"special interests" and, 45,
52–53, 55–57
Campaign finance laws, 43, 55–59
Campaign spending
impact of corporate monies,
75–78
independent expenditures,
49–50, 61
indirect expenditures, 51–53
Progressives and, 44–45
regulation, 46–47
Canada, 22, 37
Cantwell v. Connecticut (1940), 94
Carter, Jimmy, administration, 202
Cassidy, William, 174–175, 178–
179, 182
Catholicism, 103–104, 123, 124,
126
Cell phones, 191, 198
Chaffetz, Josh, 193
China, 31, 84, 207
Christmas displays, 103, 106–108
Church of England (Anglican
Church), 104, 123
CIA, 204–205
*Citizens United v. Federal Election
Commission* (2010), 42–70, 71,
73, 75–77, *76*, 81
Civil War (US), 99

Clements, Jeffrey D., 70–81
Clinton, Bill, 209
Clinton, Bill, administration,
176–177
Clinton, Hillary, 43, 60, 207, 211
Cloud computing, 215
"Coercion test", 106, 108
Cold War, 39
Common Cause (organization), 45
Communication Assistance for
Law Enforcement Act of 1994,
209
Communism, 39
Company confidentiality policies,
28
ComputerWorld (magazine), 207
Connecticut, Cantwell v. (1940), 94
Connecticut, Griswold V. (1965),
186, 188n2
Constitutional Convention of
1787, 14, 124
Contraception, 186
Coons, Chris, 97
Cooper, Elise, 201–205
Corporations
creation of corporate rights, 78
defined, 72–73
election spending, 43, 46–52,
57–58, 70–81
First Amendment rights, 42–81
history of corporate power, 80
privileges versus rights, 73–75
statistics on income, 74
See also Campaign contribu-
tions; Campaign spending
Corrections Corporation of
America, 179
Craig, Greg, 160
Creationism, 117–118
Cricket (company), 210
Croly, Herbert, 44

Protestants, 123, 126
religious hatred, 40
religious knowledge, 125–128
Sikhs, 128
teacher training and, 130–131
See also Freedom of religion;
　Separation of church and state
Religious Right, 139
Reproductive rights, 105, 186, 187
Restrepo, Sandy, 180
Reynolds v. United States (1878), 94
RFIDs (Radio Frequency
　Identifications), 198
Rhode Island, 123–124
Right of association, 186
Right to petition government, 18
Right to privacy. *See* Privacy rights
Roberts, John, 61, 72, 104, 105,
　190, 193
Robertson, Geoffrey, 83
Roe v. Wade (1973), 105
Roe, Whalen v. (1997), 187, 188n4
Roeder, Scott, 29
Roosevelt, Eleanor, 36
Roosevelt, Teddy, 51
Rosen, Jeffrey, 189–193
Rosenbloom, Rachel, 175
Roth, Jim, 203
Ruby Slippers (organization), 176
Rumsfeld, Hamdi v. (2004), 150
Rushdie, Salman, 37
Rwanda, 23

S
SAFETY Act of 2009, 209
Sanchez, Julian, 206–211
Sanders, Bernie, 159
Satanic Verses (Rushdie), 37
Saudi Arabia, 36
Scalia, Antonin, 72, 104, 105, 109,
　190, 195
Schools. *See* Public schools

Schumer, Charles, 64–65
Search warrants, 154–155, 189–
　193, 196–199, 202
Sease, Grace, 175, 182
Second Treatise of Government
　(Locke), 14–15
Sedition, 27
Self-Incrimination Clause of the
　Fifth Amendment, 186
Separation of church and state
　equal access concept and, 113
　Establishment Clause of First
　　Amendment and, 124–125
　"faith-based partnerships" and,
　　108, 141–142
　historical and constitution sup-
　　port, 96–101
　public opinion, *107*
　public schools and, 95
　state aid to religious schools
　　and, 111
　US Supreme Court justices and,
　　105
　value, 141–142
　See also Freedom of religion;
　　Public schools; Religion
Sexism, 26, 86
Sexual conduct, 19
Sexual relations, 186
Sexual torture, 83
Sikhs, 128
Silent meditation, 115
Simpson, Steve, 42–69
Sixth Amendment (US
　Constitution), 15
Sixth Circuit Court of Appeals, 118
Skating on Stilts (Baker), 203
Slaves, 65, 124
Smart dust devices, 197
Smart phones, 191
Snow, Thomas, 179